Teaching in The Spirit

Guiding our Children on the
Journey of Self-discovery

STEPHEN F.C. PORTER

Copyright © 2017, Stephen F.C. Porter
Published by Stephen F.C. Porter

No part of this book may be reproduced, stored in a retrieval system, or transmitted in any form or by any means, electronic, mechanical, or otherwise, without written permission from the author. To request permission, please contact Stephen at stephenfcporter@yahoo.com.

Scripture verses used in the text are from *The Holy Bible, King James Version*. Cambridge Edition: 1769; *King James Bible Online*, 2017. www.kingjamesbibleonline.org.

Front Cover Art © abstract412 via 123RF Stock Photo
Back Cover Photo © serrnovik via 123RF Stock Photo
Title Page Art © germina via 123RF Stock Photo
Cover and Interior Designed and Formatted by Woven Red Author Services, www.WovenRed.ca

Teaching in the Spirit/Stephen F.C. Porter—1st edition
ISBN ebook: 978-0-9959603-1-2
ISBN print book: 978-0-9959603-0-5

Author's Note: As a special needs teacher for more than twenty years, I experienced much that was honourable in the teacher profession and much that indicated that public education had somehow strayed far from it's original intent. This book is intended to suggest there is an alternative to what is being done now, that may pave the way to a better future for our children. Many of my personal experiences are included in the mix. While the events are true, names, places and times have been altered to protect the individual's privacy.

*To all our children
and their children's children*

Table of Contents

Chapter On: The Art of Easing Happiness into School 11

Chapter Two: Ending the Taboo 15

Chapter Three: Why Are We Afraid of Spirituality? 18

Chapter Four: What's the Matter with Kids Today? 21

Chapter Five: When We All Win 24

Chapter Six: The Rules of The Game 27

Chapter Seven: Educating the Heart 30

Chapter Eight: Being Kind to Yourself 34

Chapter Nine: Dualities 38

Chapter Ten: Is Their Universe Expanding? 41

Chapter Eleven: What Is Truth? 44

Chapter Twelve: True Wisdom 47

Chapter Thirteen: The Secret of Success 50

Chapter Fourteen: A Good Start 54

Chapter Fifteen: Hey Teacher, Where's My Sand Table? 57

Chapter Sixteen: Self Esteem Vs. Ego 59

Chapter Seventeen: For All We Know 62

Chapter Eighteen: Cultivating the Soil........................... 65

Chapter Nineteen: Savouring the Moment..................... 68

Chapter Twenty: Gratitude 71

Chapter Twenty-One: A Moment of Peace..................... 75

Chapter Twenty-Two: Compassion 101.......................... 78

Chapter Twenty-Three: Leading to Truth 82

Chapter Twenty-Four: Visualization 85

Chapter Twenty-Five: Don't Just Do Something, Sit There....... 88

Chapter Twenty-Six: Getting the Connection................. 91

Chapter Twenty-Seven: The Joy of Walking.................. 94

Chapter Twenty-Eight: The Myth of Good and Bad 97

Chapter Twenty-Nine: Walking in Beauty 100

Chapter Thirty: The Apple Orchard Syndrome 103

Chapter Thirty-One: Breaking Down the Garden Wall......... 106

Chapter Thirty-Two: Lightening Up 109

Chapter Thirty-Three: What Is Really Best for Them?........... 113

Chapter Thirty-Four: Letting Go of The Reins 116

Chapter Thirty-Five: The Wonder Years 120

Chapter Thirty-Six: Silence.. 123

Chapter Thirty-Seven: Remembering the Sacred.................. 126

Chapter Thirty-Eight: Before You Take Another Step............ 129

Chapter Thirty-Nine: What Do Your Children See? 132

Chapter Forty: How Do You See the Child? 135

Chapter Forty-One: Can You Hear Me? 137

Chapter Forty-Two: Pass the Bottle 140

Chapter Forty-Three: When We Belittle 143

Chapter Forty-Four: Who Are We Really Trying to Correct? .. 146

Chapter Forty-Five: A Word About Words 149

Chapter Forty-Six: Do You Think They Really Like Me? 151

Chapter Forty-Seven: Returning to The Garden.................... 154

Chapter Forty-Eight: Working with Parents.......................... 157

Chapter Forty-Nine: Be as A Child 160

Chapter Fifty: Teaching the Teacher..................................... 163

Chapter Fifty-One: All We Are Saying 166

Chapter Fifty-Two: A Word About ADD And ADHD 173

Chapter Fifty-Three: Freeing the Arts 176

Chapter Fifty-Four: Enough Already 180

Chapter Fifty-Five: Thank You for The Music........................ 184

Chapter Fifty-Six: Opening Up the Field 188

Chapter Fifty-Seven: The Living World 191

Chapter Fifty-Eight: For the Love of The Mother 194

Chapter Fifty-Nine: Every Day Is Earth Day 197

Chapter Sixty: The School in The Community 200

Chapter Sixty-One: The Value of Service 203

Chapter Sixty-Two: The Wisdom of The Elders 206

Chapter Sixty-Three: The Mind and The Media 209

Chapter Sixty-Four: Rewiring the Brain 213

Chapter Sixty-Five: The Power of Touch 217

Chapter Sixty-Six: When School Becomes Home 220

Chapter Sixty-Seven: Who Do We Think They Are? 223

Chapter Sixty-Eight: The Word Is Not Reality 226

Just One More Thing: The End Is the Beginning 228

About the Author 233

It All Starts Here

The Beatles once observed, "We all want to change the world". That's a nice idea and there aren't many folks who wouldn't do their bit to make this planet a better place, but I need to burst your bubble right now. Although there are people making a difference through courageous and selfless acts, this Earth is still riddled with the same struggles it's had since humanity graced its surface. The truth is, as long as people have a comfortable life they feel little motivation or need for change. That's a hard mindset to shift.

Maybe, you were hoping for better news. Perhaps you were hoping you could make that big difference people talk about. The good news is, things can turn and you can be part of it. Only the big changes won't come from you. The tiny ones will. This world won't transform in your lifetime, but if you believe there is a better way to live, and are ready to start demonstrating this to your kids in everything you do, each moment of each day, that shift will happen.

There is one caveat. You need to let go of any need for gratification. Instead, know from the deepest place inside of you, that all you are doing will awaken hidden knowledge. When others act from that same place, it will touch everyone with whom it comes into contact.

So you will not be hurtling into your classroom like a knight on a quest, challenging everything in place. Losing your job is not the best way to have a positive influence on your kids. Instead, as you work your way through these pages, see what resonates and might be a fit for your own approach. Then try it out. If that works out all right, take a shot at something else. Hopefully you have a long career ahead of you. This means you have time on your side. I implore you though, if you really think the time is ripe for a new paradigm in education, and you do want to make that positive difference we all talk about, please start now. Don't put it off due to fear or because it looks like too much trouble. And even though you don't need fulfillment, I assure you, somewhere when you least expect it, it will be there.

CHAPTER ONE

The Art of Easing Happiness into School

> Many run about after happiness like an absent-minded man hunting for his hat, while it is in his hand or on his head.
>
> —James Sharp

I want to start with a brief assignment. Sit back, relax, and reflect on the people you encounter in a typical day. They could be friends, family, work mates. Then, include some familiar faces, the ones you see on the TV, magazines or billboards. Check out the folks you pass on the street. Now, step back, take a deep look and consider this question: How much happiness did you find out there? How many folks radiate contentment and delight? Okay that's a tall order. How about just a little *joie de vivre*? Hold that thought.

Now, let's shift our approach. This might be less of a challenge. Observe the number of people you see rushing around plugged into mobiles, or dashing to get to meetings. Consider the road rage on our highways. Stand at the coffee machine or sit in the staff room on a Monday morning and listen to the complaints. Go for a walk in the park on a beautiful fall day and notice the how many people are texting or taking selfies, oblivious of their surroundings. I'm pretty sure that's not happiness you're witnessing.

You might say this isn't fair, people aren't always at their best when they're busy or at work. Maybe at home or on holiday it's different. Besides, how can we know what others are feeling? Guess what? If it doesn't come through in everyday life, it's not likely there. This all sounds like a cynical approach to life, but the truth often stings a bit.

So what is happiness? If you ask people if they're happy they may say, "Yeah, I'm okay," or "I get by". Their happiness equation may include family, kids, a good job, a house, a car, vacations, nice food, and clothes. Perhaps, they also have a contentment prescription which involves a lottery win or promotion.

That's all fine, but is that really happiness? What happens when things go awry, when we don't have all of that? Do we go to pieces? If life is stripped to the bone, can we still be totally fine with where we are?

You see, we confuse pleasure and happiness. In reality, they don't have much to do with each other. Pleasure comes from the outside, and while there's nothing wrong with that, it's conditional. You feel good because of something that's happened or has been achieved. Happiness is different, it comes without conditions. It lives on every level, from the inside, the outside and everywhere in between. It endures, regardless of circumstances. When life goes off the rails, we're still fine. That's probably why it's so rare. We have glimpses when we hold our babies, walk in nature or hear a moving piece of music. It's available all the time. The problem is, we're often too occupied with other things to see it.

So we buy into the illusion that something out side of us can make us happy. We go into the world searching for joy, and pass the torch to our kids, telling them pleasure and success will make them happy. We encourage them to work hard, get good marks, and later, a good job. We tell them if they find the right partner they'll drive into the sunset to their beautiful home, to live forever in bliss. Again, nothing wrong in principle, except it's only a fraction of the truth.

That's how we prepare our kids for adult life and its quest for something, somewhere out there, that will create happiness. Let's shatter a huge misconception right now; the pursuit of happiness is

The Art of Easing Happiness into School

a myth, even if it is enshrined in the U.S constitution. You can never find it by looking for it and it's time we stopped duping our kids into believing they can.

There's always something to strive for. By the time we leave school this becomes our motivation in life. We begin to believe if we work hard we'll eventually get everything we want and the more we squeeze out of life, the happier we'll be.

This logic doesn't work. Things don't have the power to make us happy. If that were so, everyone would be happy with the same things, and of course, that isn't true. When we look for happiness around the next bend, we find it isn't there, so we need to look a bit further.

Before our children get on this treadmill, we have the chance to help them understand that true contentment is available at any time, if we just recognize it. We have the keys to show them how to open the door. All those physical pleasures are meant to be used, played with and enjoyed, but when we depend on them, we're doomed to disappointment, because they always fall short.

Infants don't run around searching for happiness, they instinctively know it's right there, in anything they are doing. Educators have the chance to re-open our kids to those simple wonders of existence, the joy of seeing contentment in the here and now.

This can be done very subtly on every level of the school day. While it's great to enjoy special events, and celebrate holidays and other occasions, we can show our kids to value the ordinary and appreciate each and every day.

As a teacher, I'd be lying to say that I didn't count the days to summer break on many occasions. But there comes a point when you start to see each day as its own gift. You realize spending your days waiting for something better to come along is the direct road to heartbreak. Unfortunately, it's one that's played out by too many people, because it's how society is conditioned. It's tragic that for some, the key to true happiness only gets discovered later in life, as the number of days starts to dwindle.

What can we do in the class? On the practical level we can try to shake things up. Break from our love affair with routines. Special activities can be done on any given day. Does art class always have to be at the same time each week? Are only two gym periods allowed per week because that's what's on the schedule? Being flexible and open requires using all of our resourcefulness, but moving into the creative is what this is all about. When we allow imagination and creativity to flow, we turn even the most mundane into an adventure. It's about making each time of the day and week a comfortable place to be, a place where there can be surprises and fun, even at the most unorthodox times. Add spice into the ordinary. Surprise kids out of their lethargy.

I'm not suggesting we can turn every moment of school into Disneyland. We first need to unlearn many habits and break away from our patterns. The problem is, many educators and parents see no benefit in adopting a new template in education. In the meantime, as an individual, you can start by developing a lighter touch. Crazy as it seems, today's Order of Operations lesson can be fun when you use your imagination and stop being so serious.

Don't discount a little social down time either. Time spent experiencing the fun of hanging and interacting with friends can never be considered wasted. Open the window and let the breeze in. Stop and watch the snow falling, or a spring thunderstorm. Let kids know the world is an amazing place.

It's time we were in a bit little less of a hurry to accelerate education. Why is recess eliminated in middle, and high school? Even adults have their coffee breaks. Teachers today feel so pressured, they're afraid to stop or even slow down. Once in a while have the courage and vision to just stop and announce, "Hey gang, we've been working too hard. Let's take ten minutes, and then get back to it." Creativity goes beyond your lessons; it's woven into the entire fabric of the day, and can make life at school a constant surprise. Be on your guard to catch the little events during the day which can be a springboard for learning and fun.

Happiness is available in this moment, and it needn't come with whistles and bells. It just requires us to open our eyes and see it.

CHAPTER TWO

Ending the Taboo

> Our whole knowledge of the world, is in a sense, self-knowledge.
>
> —Alan Watts, *The Book*

In 1966, Alan Watts wrote the classic, *The Book: On the Taboo Against Knowing Who You Are*. It was a kind of manual which reflected on the mysteries of life and how we bury truth under a barrage of illusions. Watts said it was something a father might slip to his son or daughter as they entered adulthood. It became a bible for the youth movement of the time. I recall sitting up many evenings with friends, knocking back some bottles of wine, while deliberating over each point. Mr. Watt's general message, was that society taboos self-discovery and reflection, and we encourage our children to blindly follow the established patterns, rather than moving out of the game and finding their own path.

He suggested that society abhors social upheaval. So we preach what was good enough for our parents and their ancestors is good enough for everyone. If we continue to follow in the footsteps of those who walked before, we'll have a stable society which works for the good of all. In short, for society to remain unchallenged, everyone needs to stay asleep. Then we can continue to stumble along in our particular chimera of life, without questioning the system. Don't rock the boat and don't make waves. The education system of today is perfectly suited for this philosophy. It's been said that television is the opiate of the masses. It then follows that education, as it stands, is Novocain for youth. If a child comes into the system with a free-thinking and untamed spirit, give him a few years of being told what's best for him and how to fit in with society, and it'll soon be subjugated. While teaching has become more progressive in recent decades, we are still working within an old belief system which shackles our children's vision.

The sad truth is, by the time many students finish high school, they couldn't produce an original thought if their lives depended on it. Liberated thinking is tolerated in the school system, but only within the conventional norms of society. It's like a game of chess; you can make your own moves, but you have to play according to the rules. The conundrum for free thinking educators is, "How do we move outside the game, without upsetting the board?"

As someone who taught "exceptional" children, I was often able to work somewhat outside the box. Although the primary mandate was to follow the curriculum, our unique circumstances permitted me to step beyond conventional teaching. To be honest, most principals were so happy to not have to deal with the difficult kids, they usually avoided our wing of the school. That gave me the chance to give my kids what they really needed, which often lay past the sacred cube. Quantity of "learning" took second place to quality of school life. If kids were able to come to school, a place which had often been hostile to them, and go home afterwards feeling they had enjoyed their day, knowing they were important and even valued; then our day was a resounding success. I figured out very early in my career that this was not about changing or fixing anyone, but rather creating an environment where children felt accepted for being who they are; where they were given the tools to become the best version of themselves they could be. While mistakes were made, forgiveness was unconditional. Strengths were nurtured. When choices brought pain, a new way was suggested, sometimes strongly, but free of judgment. Another path was shown, perhaps ending on a happier note.

The mainstream classroom teacher can also help kids move towards a more creative experience. Don't be afraid to give students some input when you are planning the day. When you sense there is excitement over an activity, be in less of a hurry to move on. Build on the enthusiasm and let it carry over to the next endeavour. When something doesn't seem to be creating a spark, ask the kids why they aren't enjoying it. What would make it more interesting? While I'm not suggesting they run the show, their insight may add a welcome spark to your program. In everything you do, help your kids shed the skin of convention and discover the extraordinary.

When they're ready, encourage them to examine and challenge commonly accepted beliefs and philosophies. Question everything; not with a view to tear down society, but with the vision and curiosity to realize there are alternatives to what they've been told. When kids come up with radical ideas, discuss them openly. Don't be afraid to let them state how they feel, even if it goes against your own beliefs. You don't need to censure them; the other kids will help soften zealotry without any prompting from you.

We need to introduce our kids to the possibility that following in our footsteps, without question, may not always be the way to go. Our duty is to help them discover who they are first, and resist our penchant for telling them what they should, or even could be. By shifting away from arrogance and moving towards honesty and truth, we are taking the steps which will begin to transform the system. While they may seem like baby steps, your vision will make you a part of a vibrant, new way of teaching and interacting.

CHAPTER THREE

Why Are We Afraid of Spirituality?

Truth has no fear

—Anthony Douglas Williams,
Inside the Divine Pattern

In the 1970' hit, "Rock and Roll Song", Valdy wrote about performing his songs of peace and spirit to a raucous, football loving, university crowd. They'd expected a rock concert and when they didn't get it, they booed him off the stage.

Spirituality often gets this kind of bad rap. Some folk will quietly humour you when the conversation comes around to matters of the numinous, while others might clearly be uncomfortable, or even hostile. Others are drawn to the spiritual, but may not have pursued it. So when there is a chance to find out more, they will likely welcome it. Many people are longing to communicate with someone who has found a wider meaning in life.

The problem is, spirituality often gets confused with religion, and while the two have some things in common, they are not the same. Adding to this confusion, book shops mix transcendental materials with "New Age" literature. This has given rise to an association between spirituality and mediums, clairvoyance, numerology and other related disciplines. I'm not here to slag all of this, but it's not where

Why Are We Afraid of Spirituality?

I want to take you. It's just that when people equate the two, preconceptions and judgments follow. When the "S" word is mentioned, some may roll their eyes and announce they don't believe in God. Let's be clear about this. Spirituality doesn't have to involve God, although it can if you'd like.

That's enough about what it isn't. Now let's talk about what it is. Spirituality by its nature, is the knowledge there is much more to life and ourselves than our senses perceive, that we are working on deeper levels than this construct we call "self" may be aware of.

Religion may have the same basic tenets at its heart, but it often falls off the rails, becoming entangled in a mass of dogma and even superstition. As history testifies, this often gets twisted into intolerance and fanaticism, and turns toxic. This isn't the fault of religion, but rather of our ego centred, fear driven way of looking at life. Throughout history, the battlefields are littered with the bodies of those who have fought for their beliefs. The idea of a vengeful, angry God is still used to excuse the most horrific crimes. In the name of so called faith, people have been imprisoned, stoned to death, blown up and burned at the stake. It's a small wonder educators decided religion has no business in classrooms. The scientific and industrial revolutions provided another reason for removing spirituality from the education system, as science was then considered to be at odds with religion. This meant teachers have to tread lightly on matters which could be perceived as being religious.

It doesn't sound encouraging, does it? But there is good news. Over the past few decades something long overdue has happened. There's been a shift, a reconciliation between science and spirituality. Many in the scientific community are re-examining the miracle of the universe and life, along with an admission there are many things which perhaps cannot be explained. Albert Einstein comfortably accommodated the scientific and mystical without incongruity. Our sense of separation and duality is now being replaced by the notion of interconnection. The Newtonian idea of a static universe governed by immutable laws, is giving way to a notion of a dynamic and intelligent creation of which we are an inseparable part.

In a child's early years, this openness to life is still strong, but as kids are continually exposed to advertising, materialism and fear, the transcendent is reduced to occasional glimpses.

TEACHING IN THE SPIRIT

The first thing we need to do is lose our fear of the "S" word and realize spirituality is no more than an acknowledgement of our whole selves, in short, truth. It has nothing to do with indoctrinating kids into a particular faith, nor does it favour or diminish anyone's beliefs or convictions. Going deeper into ourselves is the direct path to feeling whole again and making some sense of life. Clearly, trying to do this through achievements and material success doesn't work. By re-introducing our children to the spiritual, we offer them meaning. As they move into adulthood, this knowledge can be the catalyst for a more compassionate, peaceful outlook on the world.

CHAPTER FOUR

What's the Matter with Kids Today?

What's the matter with kids today?

—*Bye, Bye Birdie*

The question has been considered in song, churned over in print and pondered by adults since parents started raising children. What is the matter with our kids? Why do they act the way they do? Don't they get what we're telling them? God help future generations.

There's good reason to feel this way. The signs of Armageddon are all around. There are shootings and knifings over a new jacket or a mobile phone. Mass killings in our schools and on the street, expose the disturbed state of today's young people. All this violence shows a disregard for the value of life. So, again, we ask. Where does all of this anger come from? Do our values mean nothing? When it comes to predicting doom, adults have it all figured out. Don't we?

The truth is, if you look down through the centuries of humanity, through all of recorded history, there's nothing new about this. From the ancient Romans, straight through the Victorian age and into the present, grownups have lamented the state of youth. We keep teaching them all we know, show them how to behave, but nothing much changes. So what's the problem? Is it just possible we are the ones who don't get it?

TEACHING IN THE SPIRIT

To help us sort this out let's use a sports metaphor. Imagine you are the management of a football team. Your team has a losing season. You don't win a single game. At the end of the year, you sack the assistant coach and bring in some younger, more motivated players. To your despair, the next season winds up being pretty much the same. The losses continue to pile up. For the following campaign, you fork out big cash for some franchise players, you purchase state of the art training machines, build a spanking new stadium and give your team every kind of perk and bonus you can afford. Yet there's no change. You wonder, what's wrong with your team? Why don't they follow what you teach them? Why can't they do what you need them to?

Now the owners take a different approach. They scout around and find a proven trouble shooter to look at the club and determine what's going wrong. He examines the records, pours over field footage, and attends practices. In short order he gives his diagnosis. "You need to get new coaches and completely change your training methods. It isn't the players fault. Everything you're teaching them is wrong."

Could this be our trouble? Are we sending in the same worn out plays year after year? We all want to give our kids every advantage; chances to get ahead, more luxury, less work and the tools they need to succeed. We give them the benefit of all we know, and they go into the world and let us down.

Our kids assume we're the ones who have it all figured out. Guess what? What if we don't? How often do we take a long look at ourselves? Are we so wrapped up in our narrow lives we've never considered there might just be a better way to live? Every so often, an advisor such as a Jesus, a Mohammed or a Buddha comes in from outside of the organization with some new ideas. The coaching staff humour them for a while and then carry on using the same old methods and bringing in worn out, predictable plays. To make matters worse, they twist those teachings to suit their own ends and pass them off as some kind of irrefutable rulebook for living.

A child's natural wisdom then becomes reprogramed with obsolete and trite ideas. We squash their natural openness, trust, creativity, spontaneity and connectedness; and replace it with half-truths. When they don't turn out the way we think they should, we point

What's the Matter with Kids Today?

and ask, "What is wrong with these kids?" With all the mirrors in this world, you'd think we'd stop and take a long hard look at our reflections. Maybe if we did, we'd realize when we impose our own views of life on our kids, we're quenching their chances of climbing out of the rut and moving toward self-realization.

So what are we supposed to do? After all, we're just teachers and parents, we can't change the world. How about we start to set our pretention aside, step back and examine what it is we're expecting our kids to emulate. Is our behaviour a role model for our kids? Do you see adults acting in a way that makes a child say, "I want to be like her?" Since we're not about to change the coaching staff, it's high time we brought in some new techniques, fresh plays and creative game plans. The ground work has already been done. We just need to get over ourselves and admit the masters were on to something. As you read on, please consider the possibility that these teachers may have had a good handle on how to play the game. Think of it as a coaching strategy makeover. You'll be surprised at how your players will rally round you.

I hope a small part of you is whispering that there is a better way to live, something you've always known it in your quieter moments. Maybe, you haven't done much about it, for fear of being burned as a witch, or worse, considered a tree hugging weirdo by your friends. Rest assured we can move in this direction together, without getting on a soapbox and alarming the neighbours.

First, you need to acknowledge the truths you already know about life. The ones you feel without the influence of the media, your friends, history, or mood of the day. Then, if you simply let it flow from you in all you do with your kids, it's unlikely anyone will have a problem with that.

CHAPTER FIVE

When We All Win

> All sentient beings should be looked upon as equal. On that basis you can gradually develop compassion for all of them.
>
> —The Dalai Lama, *Compassion*

Perhaps the most extreme example of a "winner takes all" mentality, was the High School cheerleader's mother who put out a hit on another girl because she had made the team, instead of her daughter. For those who don't recall the story, all I can say is, enough said.

Winning has become the religion of modern society. People are either winners or losers. Reality shows are based on this premise. These make great stories, but problems start when the need to win rules our personal lives.

Let's be clear. This has nothing to do with not keeping score in sporting events and "an everybody must win a trophy approach". There's nothing wrong with friendly rivalry. Yes, everyone who plays is a winner, no everyone doesn't have to get a prize. However, if we always teach in turns of win and lose, or right and wrong, it might be time to reconsider our mind-set.

Traditionally, history books have been responsible for purveying this posture. They rarely explored more than one side of an issue. There was no need.

This kind of skewed thinking runs deep. It drives politics. Religion uses it to find and manipulate followers. Without this kind of reasoning, the military would not exist. Then we fill video games, newspapers, and television with these deceptions. Spin doctors slant the news to fit the bias of their clients, or the mood of the public.

It may not be until senior school that kids are ready to explore the many sides of a story. Meanwhile, children are taught to judge, stand up and pick a side, by a society which is quick to discriminate. They are schooled in the art of choosing between good and bad. The media thrives on this culture by bringing celebrities under the microscope.

Our eagerness to judge causes suffering all around, because when we judge others, we also degrade ourselves by casting ourselves into a role which serves no one. This isn't an easy hazard to dodge, as many issues can be emotional. Obviously, we don't condone the violent and destructive actions we hear about every day. But leaping to conclusions changes nothing. If we are going to rise above constant judgment and make a positive change, we have to look deeply into events and agree there may be more to situations than we see or are told.

We can look at exemplary acts in which kids identify admirable behaviour. We also point out that we needn't be so quick to demean those who don't measure up to our expectations. Maybe there isn't always a villain. Instead we can be more uplifting; and help kids understand everyone has reasons for their actions. They may be beyond our grasp, but somehow are valid to them.

As a nation we defend ourselves when we're attacked. We also learn to be aware of, and take precautions against those who might harm us, but that doesn't make our adversaries less human than us. Exploring other's actions can help temper our own opinions, so we view events with a compassionate eye, even if we don't fully appreciate the circumstances. For those who say that's too soft, let's point out that compassion isn't always being a bleeding heart. Compassion can wield a stick. Sometimes, it takes the form of putting individuals away from society for the good of everyone, but in the end, seeks to end pain in any situation.

Young children have a huge capacity for forgiveness and kindness. When we put a label on every behaviour, that natural gift becomes faded, until our kids start reaching verdicts without ever really understanding events. We only have to look at social media to see how the world thrives on dumping their moral outrage on others.

Feeling superior to others, expressing our indignation and judging make us feel better about ourselves, but it's a backward way of doing things. This viewpoint widens the gulf between perceived ally and enemy, and takes us away from the trust we need to make a change in the world. If we look at everyone's actions in a truly empathetic, objective manner, we stand a good chance of bridging gaps.

Promote equanimity in the class. When you are looking at an historical event or story remind the kids there is more in any situation than meets the eye. This doesn't excuse bad behaviour, but we needn't be so quick to brand anyone as being "evil". Point out that non-judgment, and indifference are not the same. Contrary to what we've been told, this is not weakness. Rather, it fosters an opening and softening of the heart and goes a long way toward healing the world, in a way judgment and condemnation cannot.

Activities in the "Tribes" program, help shift kids away from the traditional "win-lose" philosophy into a "win-win" attitude. If you haven't got one, I recommend the investment. If you have dusty copy on your shelf, start flagging the activities you would like to try with your class.

We can help our children practice deep looking and listening to look beyond affairs and try to understand what drives people. Help them realize how their lives could have played out given different circumstances. Read stories of children brought up in situations completely removed from their own. Ask them how they might react to those conditions. Try role play. It furthers our own growth when we look beyond the obvious and truly "see".

CHAPTER SIX

The Rules of The Game

> Out beyond the ideas of right and wrong doing, there is a field. I'll meet you there.
>
> —Rumi

Whenever two or more people get together, rules are bound to follow. There are rules for relationships. Governments have their policies. Board games have instruction booklets. Political correctness drives behaviour in the workplace. People are good at rule making. Since humans started to hang around together, individuals have assumed charge, imposed laws, and created consequences, believing it will regulate behaviour.

If the crime rate increases, people claim society is too permissive and we need more law and order, even though it's been proven that prisons do little to correct behaviour. Rather, they become revolving doors for those with no sense of purpose. Gun control is a positive step towards decreasing street violence, however it isn't enough to insulate someone from a life of crime.

Nations have imposed their will through totalitarian regimes, only to watch them collapse under their own bureaucracy. Peace keeping forces do their best to keep troubled areas of the world stable, but that only manages a crisis. It doesn't reach underlying issues.

TEACHING IN THE SPIRIT

Historically, schools have struggled with the issue of discipline. During the first part of the 20th century, strict and usually unbendable rules were imposed, in the belief it would produce obedient children who would later grow up to become model, productive citizens. When it was suggested free thinking was being stifled, a sharp shift occurred. Harsh order gave way to a more flexible approach, based on the more enlightened belief that children need to discover their own path to self-regulation and learning.

Time shows neither paradigm effectively altered inherent behaviour. Now as violence has become rampant in some schools, there is again a cry for stricter controls. Many schools resemble armed prisons, replete with metal detectors and police presence.

So what's the problem with law and order? Simply this; no matter how many laws we impose on society, our schools included, it's never enough, because change needs to come from inside each of us. Imposing will from above does nothing more than put bandages on raw sores. The idea we can alter long term behaviour through force is an example of wrong thinking. Only when we see ourselves differently, can true change happen.

The Buddha insisted we all have the potential to become Buddhas; to awaken to our innate decency and integrity. However, we've become so smothered by the illusions we believe about life, that we need to be constantly reminded of this basic goodness. On the other hand, something amazing happens when we help children see their true nature. They start to see they are totally okay and they have nothing to prove. There is one caveat though. As mentors, we have to discover this within ourselves before we can pass it on to them.

As we become more in touch with what we really are, we start to knock down the myths which make up our society. We become more closely connected with basic truth. As people become more self-realized and aware, they naturally treat others with compassion, because it's the natural state. When children see their purpose in life has nothing to do with society's ideas of success, they no longer find it necessary to put on a show of bravado. They realize who they are is fine, and they can be themselves and start to reveal that goodness.

It's clear that by imposing severe and inflexible, or even intimidating discipline, we do nothing to help our kids find their way. We might be able to manage our classes and keep order, but if it's only because children fear the consequences. It can't create the kind of self-regulation which will hold them in good stead for a lifetime.

This doesn't mean we're going to tear down all the rules and structure, and let mayhem rule. You only have to read "Lord of the Flies" to get a glimpse at what happens when children with no sense of self, are left without direction. As long as we continue to be disconnected from our true nature, we will carry on acting badly at times and will still need outside direction.

As adults, as we become more okay with our real nature and start to drop our games and self-importance, we'll feel less need to control, and we can begin to relax our rules with children. In turn, as they start to connect with their inner wisdom and become more cognizant, they will view life with more equanimity. Once this connection is made and they feel more at ease with themselves, their actions will be directed from a deeper place.

This way of living can be passed forward to others with little effort, as people learn better by example than from preaching. It's not wishful thinking. People have learned how to act badly through the modelling of others, and positive change can work the same way. It will take time, so it makes sense to get started today.

CHAPTER SEVEN

Educating the Heart

> Here one needs a more balanced approach to life. It is not all about one's job, or how much money one makes.
>
> —The Dalai Lama,
> Lecture: *On the Buddhist Path to Peace* (1988)

At this point I think it's fair to make a few comments about the mainstream education system. Its primary mandate is to prepare youth to move into the working world and it would be hard to dispute that the best way to do this is to give kids the facts and skills needed to prepare for a career. This is all fine, but while we are guiding our kids towards success in the 21st century, when it comes to educating the whole child, our modus operandi is stuck in the past. While this approach may fulfil the mission, it does little to help children discover themselves and learn about life.

We love working with kids and want to help them become the best version of themselves they can be, but the demands of the current system mean there's little space for children to explore who they are. This doesn't sound positive.

Educating the Heart

It would be helpful to know that someone, somewhere out there is blazing a new trail for us. There must be examples of more progressive approaches to education, where schools are guiding youth to discover their true goodness and potential. It's not an easy sell. After all, you won't find many business institutes which emphasize empathy and kindness. When a prospective lawyer moves towards his goal of reaching the Bar, he is rarely reminded how loving compassion can help ease the suffering of future clients.

This is truly a shame, because instilling these values takes nothing away from the program, when it is blended with training for the workplace. When we educate the whole student, we help them find more real meaning in their future careers, plus, we spark their desire to make a difference in the world, one which has nothing to do with personal gain.

That's where the good news comes. There are schools which are doing exactly that. Many of the alternative elementary schools offer a more complete approach to learning, and this is spreading the awareness that education needs to be more than just a training ground for future employment.

Post public education centres such as Oneness University in India have the education of both spirit and mind at their core.

The Dalai Lama Centre for Peace and Education in Vancouver, British Columbia is working to advance education which addresses the full capacities of children. This centre was founded in 2005 with the intent of ensuring that the teaching of mindful awareness and compassion be embedded as a basic component of both primary and secondary education.

It is a non-religious, non-political centre that the Dalai Lama says will, "Develop the heart, be compassionate, work for peace in the heart and in the world."

If this school worked in isolation, its affect might be nominal, but it doesn't end there. The aim is to grow to become a vital part of the community and then expand beyond that. The Dalai Lama says, "When our community is in a state of peace, it can share that peace with neighbouring communities." Students will be part of an educational environment which not only cultivates mindfulness, but encourages heightened awareness within diverse practices of the arts. At the same time, it will provide the skills necessary for students entering the workplace. After all, the modern world continues to turn regardless of one's degree of enlightenment.

Strong connections will be developed with schools to help them design programs which encourage the emotional, social and moral development of educators and their students. It will become international in its reach and connections, through association with prominent researchers and agencies such as the Collaborative for Academic, Social and Emotional Learning (CASEL) in the U.S.

Currently, the Holistic Life Foundation out of Baltimore, Maryland is breathing new life into the public system by introducing mindfulness, compassion and meditation practices to students, particularly those in challenged areas. Their *Holistic Me*, after school program features meditation, awareness and Yoga training to help connect students to relaxation, conflict resolution and improved focus and concentration. In addition, it features enrichment activities such as Makers Space, Woodworking, Environmental, Team Building, Art & Entrepreneurship, Basketball, Martial Arts, Dance, Steel Drums, and STEM.

Mindful Moment exercises are performed each morning in participating schools, during which instructors mentor students in meditation techniques. An amazing, and to me ground breaking concept, is the Mindful Moment Room, which gives students experiencing challenges on any given day, a chance to sit peacefully in a quiet space and centre themselves. In higher grades older students are taught to mentor younger ones.

It is this kind of enlightened programming which can help put real meaning into the education of our children. If more of these progressive practices make their way into our schools, we might see administrators and programmers wake up to the amazing possibilities teaching the whole child can offer to our youth.

These may be small steps in the move to teach holistically. Our education system won't change overnight. Its roots are mired too deeply. But alternative, holistic foundations such as these can be portals to a new way of looking at education. As they become integrated into the community, they become the catalyst needed for society to accept a new paradigm in education, where spirituality and education can become companions in young people's lives.

In the meantime, in our classrooms, we can incorporate these basic ideals, by emphasizing selflessness in our actions. We can help remind students that by being mindful in all they do, they will be more able to act skilfully and compassionately. Children can discover there is nothing to be gained from success if it is only from a monetary standpoint, and a truly rewarding career is not self-interested, it centres on reaching out to co-workers and clients at all times. By teaching the same skills and knowledge from these vantage points, higher education will begin to have greater meaning and will enrich the lives of generations to come.

If you would also like to see how a truly democratic, student based school can work, I suggest the following classic:

A.S. Neill *Summerhill School: A New View of Childhood American Edition*. New York: St. Martin's Press 1992

CHAPTER EIGHT

Being Kind to Yourself

> Be gentle, patient, humble and courteous to all, but especially, be gentle and patient with yourself.
>
> —H L Sidney Lear,
> *A Dominican Life Artist: A Sketch in The Life of
> The Reverend Pere Besson of The Order of St. Dominic*

If you believe your heart could use a little warming and opening, watch kindergarten kids. You might be surprised at just how kind and caring they can be to each other. Of course, there's the occasional squabble when two of them want the same toy, and that's where the teacher, with the wisdom of Solomon, helps find a happy ending. A lot of primary school is about learning to share, talk politely and help friends. You'll find that most kids have a pretty good handle on these basics of life.

The problem is, as they get older, move through high school and finally into the work world, some of these ideals get put on the back burner. It would be nice to assume the principles instilled in primary grades are ingrained enough to carry over into the teenage years and then beyond. The reality is, as life goes on and the going gets tougher, it's harder to maintain and extend altruism. Many people have their hands too full just holding on to what they have, to start reaching out. Even in adult life, much of society's civility is merely the political correctness needed to survive and get ahead, and has little sincerity behind it.

Did you ever consider that one of the reasons we are unable to always be selfless in our approach to life, is that we have never learned how to be kind to ourselves? If we constantly feed ourselves material and mental toxins and if we're mired in guilt, we have little chance of extending the milk of human kindness to others. The plain truth is, when we're completely full of ourselves, we have little space for anyone else.

Along life's road, we learn some things are good for us and others are not. When you're a kid, you're taught that filling up with candy is not a good thing. Later, it's alcohol, smoking and drugs that can do harm. We're encouraged to move away from the television and get exercise. Meanwhile, we pay little heed to our mental state, which is incessantly bombarded with influences which poison our outlook on life.

Advertising tells kids they need to have bigger and better everything to be happy. Ads not only encourage us to eat badly and excessively, but equate eating with happiness. Many video games and TV shows devalue human life, reinforce the myth of good and evil, and glamourize rampant materialism.

All of these notions ebb away at our kid's self-concept, as they're fed a constant diet of deceptions. These messages do nothing but diminish human value. The sad fact is, no matter what we do at school, our influence over what our children's experience at home is limited.

That is why it's so important to do whatever we can at school to help our kids realize their basic goodness, and understand when they're kinder to themselves, it's easier to deal with others in a gentler way.

When the children are sitting in circle at the start of the day, (any age is suitable), they can affirm a couple of ways in which they can be caring to themselves and their friends that day. They might assure their peers that it's okay to make a mistake. Or they may make a promise to help their classmates, or to share. Sometimes all that's needed is a reminder to live the day with a little more consideration. This needn't be a warm, fuzzy, hug fest; just a group of friends who know that since they're all in it together, they might as well help each other to move along the way.

Later, we can start to take a critical look at the input we're receiving every day. Kids may want to volunteer some of the negative and destructive comments they've found on social media, and discuss what they think motivates people to think like this.

Older kids can be encouraged to talk about some of the things they may have seen on television the night before. They can look at the attitudes displayed on the shows and discuss whether this is the way things really are. At an age when marketing has its strongest sway, it's a good time to examine what advertisers are dishing out, and how they get us to buy.

Is there anything wrong with a fast food dinner once in a while? No. Is eating a steady diet of McDonalds and pizza a good idea? That's a different story. Are commercial manufacturers trying to sell happiness? Is a cell phone a useful tool? No doubt about that. But is it improving our lives to walk around glued to our phones, while we miss the world going by? Is it realistic to think the latest electronic gadget will make us happy? All of these are springboards for discussions in which children can be encouraged to think about the quality of life offered by materialism. It's crucial for us to take a look at how we're teaching these kinds of life skills to kids. By simply rhyming off the things which are bad, we do nothing to help them make better choices.

Then how can we start instilling in them the importance of being kind to themselves in everyday life? It's really quite simple. By looking head-on at the kinds of lifestyles we embrace, and truly evaluating their worth, we can equip kids with the tools they need to make conscious decisions, rather than the mindless ones, consumers make every day.

Negative self-image is not a permanent tattoo. We can help change patterns by the way we model our own behaviour and with the kind of open dialogue we promote in class. Kids need to be encouraged to say something positive about themselves and each other. At a time when there is so much emphasis on academic prowess and success, many children feel inferior if they can't measure up to what parents and teachers expect of them. Teachers have to be quick to point out the positive qualities they see in each child and help each one to see these in themselves. Mindfulness is the key. If you are truly aware of everything that's going on in your class, you come to know your students on many levels. You notice the small improvements and the progress every child makes.

Sometimes it's important to announce it to the whole group. At other times it's more appropriate to have a private word with a student, to let her know you noticed something she did, and that you appreciate it. When you've taken the time to truly see your students, you will instinctively know what to do. This just might be a huge step in preventing the downward spiral of inferiority which starts when children are young; one from which they may never recover.

All of this can be incorporated into the regular routine of the day. We don't need a "Let's all feel good about ourselves" session. All we need to do is be constantly aware of the amount of mental contamination our kids are exposed to each day, and help to minimize or reverse its effect.

CHAPTER NINE

Dualities

A circle only has one side: basic geometrical concept.

When people start voicing their opinions you're not likely to find a lot of grey. You'll have no problem finding the black and white, but that area in between often requires you to dig in and do some deeper excavation. People love to get their point across. You must know the kind of person who starts his sentence with, "Let me tell you something!" From there the conversation becomes pretty much one sided.

Newspapers love to print headlines, screaming outrage and judgment at every opportunity. The internet is full of jaded, bitter, people spewing out venom in the guise of sharing their views. The public is quick to pronounce sentence on those whose ideas or lifestyles don't match their own. We're constantly told to choose a side, stand for something, not back down.

Of course, we have our preferences, our views, and we make a stand when we see injustice. But sometimes that only carries us half way to the truth. If we simply rush into judgment and close the door to the full story, we do a disservice to ourselves and others. Ultimately, there is a lot less black and white in this world than we think. And while we sometimes will take sides, we can't just ignore all that

Dualities

space in between. When we're fixated with being right all the time, then our actions are obscured by bias and intolerance.

Our insistence on looking at everything in terms of dualities is one of the chief stumbling blocks to reaching the truth. When we look at everything in black and white, right and wrong, and similar polarities; we tend to develop a very narrow vision of the world. We expect things to fit into distinct slots, with little room for deviation. It's amazing how narrow minded we can be at times. I see it in myself every time the topic of food comes up. "Ugh, how can you eat Brussel sprouts?" or music, "How can you listen to that?"

One of the major notions we adults cling to is the distinction between grown up and child. Adults often tend to regard children as if they were a separate species. Many feel their longevity is enough to qualify them as life coaches. Of course, kids have a lot to learn and we can help them with that. You don't reason with a three-year-old who is about to touch a hot stove. But often, we're guilty of forgetting children are part of the wide spectrum of humanity, and all of us, whether infant or senior, have the same basic feelings, desires and hopes as the rest of our brothers and sisters.

Does anyone really know when childhood ends? When do the rules change? For that matter, at the age of 80, does a person suddenly become labelled as helpless, in need of being coddled and patronized?

If we're going to help guide the young people in our care, we need to embrace the mind-set that kids are the same as us, only with less years spent on this earth. We may have experience to offer, but it is neither superior nor more important than anything they bring to the table.

When we start to teach the interconnectedness of all things and when we introduce true equanimity to children, the need to polarize everything vanishes. Perhaps this will help them avoid the necessity of having everything labelled in neat little packages.

This can be demonstrated with simple exercises and examples. Have kids hold up their right hand. Then hold up the left. Now have them pretend they only have one hand. Which is right and which is left? Look at a coin. There can be no head without the tail. What is hot? How can you know hot without cold? Ask them what a warm summer day feels like. Now, have them describe a warm winter's day. I'm sure you can think of dozens more.

The point is of course, everything has at least two sides. Without one, the others cannot exist. Nothing occurs in isolation, but rather, is proportional to something else. When we present this to children, they can see what they thought to be opposites or absolutes, are in fact part of an inseparable whole. By letting go of our need to see everything in black and white, our minds become more spacious, willing to take in the whole picture, rather than building a wall out of prejudice and conditioning. When we don't cling to our preferences, things become infinitely clearer.

Without the roadblock of duality, we help move our kids along the path to greater understanding and empathy.

CHAPTER TEN

Is Their Universe Expanding?

> If you cling to something as an absolute truth and are caught in it, when truth comes and knocks on the door, you will refuse to let him in.
>
> —Buddha

When we're very small, life is uncomplicated and predictable. It's an intimate world which tends to revolve around parents, significant others and the rituals of sleeping and eating. For the most part, the bigger picture isn't of much concern. Living is pretty egocentric, focused on getting needs met, and there is usually hell to pay if they are not. Naturally, if children are around a large circle of family and friends, their world will start to expand somewhat and they might become socially savvy at an earlier age.

As children reach school age, we're careful to instill and reinforce the virtues of sharing and caring for others. Their universe is growing a few steps at a time.

Yet we have to ask a very profound question about our education system, and answer it honestly. Are we continuing to aid in this process of enlarging young people's outlooks? Or are we merely filling their minds without dated ideas, narrow minded opinions and the latest technology, which will become just another part of the mind-numbing background noise which plagues them throughout their lives? With this constant input of information and stimuli, there is almost no space to take refuge and when the mind is in turmoil, there isn't much room for spacious, imaginative living.

As young people are taken into our trust, we often sell them what is safe and familiar. Is this truly what you would want for yourself if you were starting out in life? Think about yourself and those around you. Are their minds liberated, or are they mostly caught up in the drama of their personal narrow existences? How much of what we do is joyous and spontaneous, and what is merely automatic response based on past actions?

If the human race is going to start waking up and experiencing all that life has to offer, we need to begin with our children. It's time to take stock of what we are giving our kids and acknowledge much of it is an old tired paradigm, one which doesn't foster openness and creativity.

We're all so much more than our thinking and senses perceive. Every awakened being throughout history has urged us to come to this realization. But the sad fact is, we have little chance of even scratching the surface of our unlimited possibilities when we're caught up in a jumble of fears, illusions and behavioral loops.

Many times, appearances don't equal truth. Look at Terry Fox. Despite receiving a devastating blow from cancer early in his life, his faith and conviction led him to run half way across Canada with one leg. Any doubt, fear or physical pain couldn't overshadow the realization he was capable of much more than his condition suggested. Our children are well aware of Terry's story, but his is only one of the thousands of individuals who opened up their world and saw limitless possibilities, who understood that facts don't always count. We may not all be heroes, but we can leave our limited world of apprehension, presumptions, shame, and guilt; and inflate our universe, no matter what our circumstances. You don't need a guru to point this out. Take the time to introduce kids to individuals who have gone beyond the obvious and entered the astounding.

We have the marvelous opportunity to help our children truly open, grow, and clear their minds, so they can connect with everything they are. There are many simple ways to begin. How about letting them experience the joys of nature and silence? Why don't

Is Their Universe Expanding?

we help them rediscover the wonder of life and realize they are fine as they are, instead of feeling they need to prove themselves. What if we stop making them feel as though they need to be fixed? Now, their balloon is starting to inflate. We can help them see goals and dreams are an exciting part of life, but their personal worth is neither measured by, nor restricted to these. When they understand this, their lives continue to open.

While not turning them into cynics, we must allow, even encourage them to question and assess what they've been told. Give them examples of those who didn't just accept everything they were taught and went beyond the mundane to find real fulfillment. By letting them explore this wider outlook on life, there's a better chance they won't be confined to the small domain visible only through the veil of society. One moment at a time, we can point our children on their way to self-realization, and a gratification which has nothing to do with accomplishment, material success or status. They can see true reality is larger than they ever dreamed was possible. Then they can join in the dance, instead of holding up the wall.

CHAPTER ELEVEN

What Is Truth?

> Truth is not that which can be demonstrated. It is that which simplifies.
>
> —Antoine de Saint-Exupery,
> *Wind, Sand and Stars*

If you don't know where you're going it's not likely you'll get there, and if you aren't sure what you are looking for, it's going to be difficult to find. This is the conundrum we face when we talk about truth. It's often quite abstract. Facts are different. Mountains of books and pages of websites give us enough information to sound clever over a thousand dinner conversations. The trouble is, the answers to many of our deeper questions are much harder to find, because they're subjective. Delineating truth isn't so easy, and it often creates more questions than it answers.

Does life contain absolute truths? Is your truth same as your neighbours? Need it be? Are belief and truth the same? Must others share our convictions?

Those are a lot of questions stemming from such a small word. Given all this confusion, before we teach children about truth, we'd better figure out what we are talking about. Truths might be abstruse ones which involve spirituality, politics or family values. They may

What Is Truth?

be more mundane, such as common etiquette or school curriculum. The fact is, most of our convictions have been borrowed from our teachers, family and society. These may be the same ones our ancestors believed should be taught, defended, and ultimately passed on to the next generation.

What we must remember, is many of these principals are antiquated hangovers from bygone eras. When we hand them down as absolutes, we give children little credit for having their own values. In fact, we are suggesting theirs are inconsequential.

Try to imagine what kind of thinking made Victorian adults pass on their stuffy, stifling morals to their children. Yet they did so, probably with the best of intentions. The children of apartheid grew up with the biases given them by their generation. Zealots and extremists indoctrinate their young into their creed of hate from the day they are born. While these instances are extreme examples of flawed thinking, many of the subtler lifestyles we pass on are also in need of some close scrutiny. Most of our kids adopt these ideas with little question and carry them well into their adult lives.

Before you give a child your values as given facts, bear this in mind. Our personal view of reality is not absolute. Customs and motives that we find curious are commonplace in other cultures. That's why it's crucial for us to leave behind our biases, and allow children to view life with a critical eye, making their own informed decisions. When we're dogmatic with youth, we build fences around their perception. Later, they may spend years pulling them down in the search for clarity. Remember, when the mind is full of set ideas, there is little room for anything fresh and liberated.

This isn't to say that all we have built up and believe is false, nor does it mean we shouldn't expose our youth to these attitudes. But we need to present our beliefs as just that, viewpoints, not laws inscribed on stone tablets. They are guides, directions to explore, from which more knowledgeable assessments can be made.

Do we demand that kids do things our way because we have a need to control? Do we preach what merely serves us? Are the minor things we fuss about really important? Does it really matter if Johnny sits on his bum when he is in the circle? Is it worth getting into a brawl with Freddy because he takes his coat off on a winter's day while playing basketball? Maybe he's hot. If we're cold, perhaps we need to put on a warmer coat.

From the profound beliefs we hold about society and life, to the everyday activities we often turn into our own petty agendas, we must remember these notions are ones we have largely borrowed from our ancestors. So, while we have knowledge and experience to pass on, it isn't the last word. As we try to guide our children, we must always be aware the medicine which works for us may be poison to others. In the end, we need to allow our youth to look at the wide spectrum of ideologies and make their own decisions, without the yoke of dogma.

CHAPTER TWELVE

True Wisdom

> I fear that our technology has outstripped our humanity.
>
> —Albert Einstein

The age of technologically has exposed a rather glaring paradox. The past century has seen communications, medicine, science, and personal comfort grow in a way that would have great granny wondering whether she'd been kidnapped and taken to another planet. This, we can call smarts. On the other side of the coin we see the violence, greed and materialism running rampant. So what's missing from this puzzle? That missing piece is called wisdom. Insight has been devalued in favour of the accumulation of information. Intelligence and education are placed above enlightened thinking, and spirit is mostly put on the shelf where it doesn't get in the way of our pursuit of gain and pleasure.

Knowledge is power, is the catch phrase for our time. We trust that information acquired through books, the internet and education, will render us sages. However, as many educators and great thinkers realize, intelligence and knowledge do not equate to wisdom. The human ingenuity which has brought us to the pinnacle of achievement and technology is astounding. But knowledge not tempered with insight has also taken us to the brink of world-wide holocaust on more than one occasion.

It has choked Mother Earth in pollution. The inventor of DDT was awarded the Nobel Prize in the last century. Yet decades after the discovery of its devastating effects and subsequent ban, its traces can still be found in people nowhere near the areas originally sprayed. It is the so-called skill of our world leaders that has led to the enslavement of entire cultures and the starvation and want that exists in this world. Useless wars based on political and commercial ambition, such as Vietnam and Iraq, have left nations wasted and families shattered. Religious doctrines are at the root of bloody crusades and carnage.

It's common knowledge there is enough food and shelter for each person on this planet, yet the bulk of wealth and abundance rests in a few privileged countries among a handful of opportunists, while much of the world goes without. Still, for the most part, people blindly follow their leaders in the belief they can and will do the right thing.

Scientists once boldly predicted our superior intellect would carry us to Utopia. However, far from it, we have been spinning further away with each passing moment. If you take a deep look at the world which lies beyond our modern comforts, it's clear our brains have done little to bring humankind to either peace, or peace of mind. Our quest to amass facts and resources, and our drive to pursue power at all costs have brought us to the brink.

There's a myth out there which suggests a good education will lead to a satisfying career. After that you can start a family, have children, grandchildren, collect a lot of stuff along the way, and live happily ever after. Some people seem to pull it off, but I think you'll find they already have a pretty good handle on life. For the majority, this path ends up falling short. Somewhere inside, we know this equation omits a very important part. It's only with a connection to the whole of life, to truth, that real peace is possible.

Without this much ignored bit, we spin in circles, grabbing at whatever pleasure we can get, but it never meets the mark. How many corporate leaders have been busted for trying to swell their fortune by bilking their investors out of their life savings and pensions? Look at the number of people who destroy their health, their lives and the lives of others in the drive for success. If possessions made people happy, then it stands to reason everybody who has them should be happy. This isn't the case.

It all sounds grim, but the upside is that we, as educators can do something about it. If you know in your heart this simple truth, then you can reach down inside and start passing it on. This is the same message the masters have been telling us through the ages; you know, the one that says, "The Kingdom is within." This isn't to suggest we have to deny the importance of knowledge, nor need we live as ascetics. It does point out however, perhaps our idea of purpose in life is a little confused.

As teachers, we have the privilege of being able to re-open young minds and allow spirit to flourish once again. We can make our children aware there are truths they may have glimpsed when they were very young, which are still alive just below the surface. One of the biggest keys to freeing us from much of the suffering we bring upon ourselves is the knowledge we are all one, connected, and really never alone. We've also been taught happiness is right here, in the now, if we just set aside our dramas and personal stories long enough to let it in. What if we take a second look at some of these messages and admit they have the power to completely upend our way of living?

Don't be afraid of it. It isn't anything new, it's something we all know on a deeper level, but have forgotten. When we have the courage to let our children realize they can indeed have more than they've been led to believe; when they can grow up with the knowledge that life has greater choices to offer than they ever imagined; when we as educators know we have started to help our children reach out to this knowledge and they will pass it to their children, they will be on the road to living rather than just getting by.

CHAPTER THIRTEEN

The Secret of Success

> But if you do not know yourself, then you are in poverty and you are poverty.
>
> —Osho, *The Mustard Seed, The Gnostic Teaching of Jesus*

One of the oldest story lines is about a man who sells his soul to the devil in exchange for success, youth, or the modern equivalent, the corporation. Each tale, from *Faust* to *Rosemary's Baby* ended in tears. When we hear such yarns, we "get it" at the time. Still, our perceptions about success seem to be dominated by position, status and wealth, and some folks are literally willing to sell their soul to get them.

If we asked kids, parents, or educators to give the main mandate of schooling, most would probably answer that it is to prepare children for success in life. Now I don't have any problem with this idea. But let's back up a bit and ask a very important question. What is success? If we're going to help prepare children for success in life, we'd better have a clear idea about what it is, so we can point them in that direction.

Here's how the standard life algorithm goes. Studying hard at school equals good grades. High marks grant you entrance into the right university and ultimately a good job. The good job gives you the means to start a family, have a comfortable home, a nice car and other things taken for granted in western society. Now I'm not putting this down. In fact, it has the potential to lead us to a pretty decent way to live, and if part of this formula includes acquiring a bunch of junk, so be it. The problem is, this equation leaves out vital components, such as contentment, sense of connection with the world and feeling at peace with life. Feel free to fill in any pieces of this puzzle you see missing.

It takes some people longer than others to discover that the acquisition of material goods or a title doesn't guarantee the good life. Yet we continue to perpetrate the myth that a good education will eventually take us there. This is like the Santa Claus myth, you can hold on to it for a while, but in the long run it turns out to be a fraud.

In traditional Eastern philosophy, success and power aren't defined in terms of wealth and standing. Rather, they are measured in terms of moving along the path to self-realization and spiritual growth, becoming more in harmony with both ourselves and the universe of which we are part. At that point there is no one to compete with and nobody to whom we must answer. Wisdom and learning are their own ends. There isn't always a tangible prize or even a positive experience to be reached at the end, nor is one needed.

This of course, is a huge pill for much of Western culture swallow. In a society which tends to gauge success by the size of our bank books, possessions, status, and the number of friends we have on Facebook, convincing others to see that self-fulfillment and harmony are the paths which truly serve us, is a hard sell.

Now, while I understand what some anarchists are trying to say, I don't believe we need to rip apart our Western society and culture. But I would certainly suggest a few good tweaks. While a good education can indeed give us the choice of a rewarding and possibly lucrative career, we need to shift from the exclusive emphasis of these goals. Children need to experience a much wider spectrum of learning than we currently are giving them. By helping kids see the wonder of the world around them and to find joy in the simple acts in life, they can begin to understand the goal isn't reached at the end of education. Rather, it's something which grows and flourishes all along life's path.

With that solid base there's a fair chance when they go out into the world and find a career, they will be more in tune with themselves and life. As they continue to grow, they will find that happiness and prosperity live within themselves and there is nothing to prove. Whatever material success they achieve is just fine, but it won't define their worth, or be a measure of their success. The line, "I have arrived", will actually never apply, because they'll know they've always been there. This is why we need to be cautious about over emphasizing test results and quantifying the achievement of expectations.

It was only after Jimmy Carter was defeated in his attempt to retain the presidency of the United States that he truly found his path in life. Carter said that after the defeat, he was crushed and had retired to his farm to live out his days. However, when he opened to the suffering around him, he knew he could use his influence to help human kind. From there, he became involved with Habitat for Humanity program which has built houses around the world for those who otherwise would have no chance of having a home. He and his wife founded the Jimmy and Rosalyn Carter Work Project, where his family is still directly involved in the building of new homes. For many, success would be serving as President of the United States, full stop. However, for Jimmy Carter, true success came when his awareness and compassion led him to help relieve the suffering of his fellow humans.

Each day, as we help children discover their innate goodness, we start to deflate the myth that there is something out there they must achieve to give them worth. The fact is, they already have it. There is no need to continually ask children what they are going to be. They already are, and every moment of their lives carries its own brand of achievement and reward. Every time we start to evaluate our kids in terms of marks and awards, we need to stop and realize how we are also degrading them. Being aware of this doesn't mean we discount the value of achievement in school and the promise of a rewarding vocation in life. It does mean putting the person and their accomplishments in balance, giving children a perspective which can only increase self-esteem and fulfillment in their lives.

The Secret of Success

This also helps them see the honour in any profession or vocation, rather than thinking that certain positions in life are superior to others. Of course, many parents of our generation may find this tough to accept. There are few parents who would be pleased to hear their children have decided on careers as maintenance workers for the city, or servers in a restaurant. However, when we value children for who they are, we see that anything they do with dignity and dedication is okay.

When I spent some time in hospital in England, I was taken to X-ray by a man who was able to light up the entire ward by his presence. For a time, he made me forget how ill I was. When I asked him about his work, he told me when he saw his clients smile, he knew he'd done his job. This man lived success. If our children start viewing success from this perspective, they will find that achievement is attainable for anyone, not just the privileged, gifted and well educated.

Educators and parents need to spread this message every day and show children the real meaning of success. If they can enjoy the challenge of reaching goals in their life, without becoming attached to, and identifying with them, they will have truly arrived.

CHAPTER FOURTEEN

A Good Start

> Everything is a circle. We're each responsible for our own actions. It will come back.
>
> —Betty Laverdure: Ojibway Leader

When I taught Middle School, our board arranged to have an outside agency come in and teach anti-bullying to the kids; a reaction shared by many schools in response to the disturbing rise in aggressive behaviour. The kids came to the auditorium, listened attentively, completed the assignments, and performed the role playing admirably. Upon completion of the course they received a nice certificate. Do you know what happened next? Nothing. Hardly anything changed. The same kids who had been bullies, took a day off and then continued to harass and intimidate their weaker peers. Those who were victims, remained so.

Most schools today incorporate programs designed to help children learn responsible social behaviour. There are courses in anti-racism, anti-violence, sexual tolerance and equity awareness; all intended to help reduce or eliminate undesirable social conduct and in theory help kids along the road to becoming upright citizens.

While these programs are obviously well-intentioned, they ignore an important point. The fact we need these programs tells us that we've missed the mark in guiding youth at an early age, both in the home and in the school. We're trying to correct attitudes which likely have already become rooted. For whatever reason, many kids feel it necessary to express their discontent through intimidation and other forms of bullying. If we want to make a lasting change, we need to find out what's behind this and adjust the way we guide our kids before these symptoms manifest. The causes of this behavior likely run deeper than we would like to think.

With full day Kindergarten now the norm in many schools, children are starting school at an earlier age than ever before. Before that, many kids are enrolled in some form of pre-school program. The result is, kids may be walking through the doors of their first school at the age of three. We can't keep shrugging our shoulders and saying raising a child is solely the concern of the parent. The fact is, once he is in the school we also become responsible for his welfare and well-being. It's here we have this marvelous opportunity to help shape attitudes and nourish everything positive in him.

By nurturing children's self-esteem, so they actually feel good about who they are, we can largely negate their need to bully or feel they are in competition with everyone. If more programs such as "Tribes" become the mainstay of the classroom at primary ages, children will understand we're all in the same boat and there is no need for a "Get others before they get us" outlook. When co-operation, sharing and empathy become our normal way of operating, there's a good chance we won't need to fix things later on when trouble comes. We can all agree a carefully maintained car and a preventative approach to medicine, can stave off problems later. The state of our mental and spiritual health is no different. It needs to be cared for from day one.

Of course, there are many kids who grow up in areas where violence and looking out for your back are a way of life. Some children in these kinds of environments may need some pretty intense life therapy. Often, the parents are too close to see it. So this is where we need to have our eyes and ears open, look for signs and try to intervene while there is a possibility of making a difference. If support is not readily available, we need to scream loud and long until someone takes notice. Believe me, if you persist you will get results.

TEACHING IN THE SPIRIT

Parents and educators must join in advocating for more assistance, and not give up there. When we see a powerful need, we need to do all that we can to fill it. Parents must appreciate that their kid's welfare is our first concern.

Of course, it can only help to maintain the programs that address the problems which have evolved, but we also have to start at a younger age, when kids are the most receptive. Then it's easier to shift perspectives which may result in the difficulties we face in the higher grades. Remember, parents have probably also lived with a go backwards and fix-it mentality. It's essential they understand that when kids grow up viewing themselves and others in a positive light, there will be less need to deal with crisis later.

We need to make sure parents are kept aware of what's going on in the classroom. This could mean holding parent nights, and non-academic open houses which present and explain the kinds of affirmative activities we're running in the classroom. Here they can see first-hand what we are doing to help students feel positive about life and themselves, and how our approach can point them in a better direction.

Remember, we are not trying to be the parent. Let's be honest, no one wants to feel teachers think they can do a better job of raising their child. But if we show them how every child can thrive when we help them change their outlook, and if they see their child acting in a happier, more confident manner, they'll be on board with what we're doing.

Like it or not, in a time when many youth are experiencing so much conflict, parents and teachers need to share in the growth of the child. Nobody's right and no one is wrong. Together we can see that setting a shared example of caring, compassion, and supporting everything good in each child, can only serve to develop self-knowledge and a sense of grace with life. If children grow up with this view, they are much less likely to feel the need to prove their power by putting others down.

CHAPTER FIFTEEN

Hey Teacher, Where's My Sand Table?

> To a young heart, everything is fun.
>
> —Charles Dickens,
> *Perils of Certain English Prisoners*

While the first day of school is a bit scary to the neophyte, it can also be an awesome experience. After all, Kindergarten is geared to young kids, and at the age of four it's quite okay for a child to act like a child. In fact, it's encouraged. Brightly coloured posters and pictures cover the walls. The low, comfy furniture is built with kids in mind. There might be strange and wonderful plants, and sometimes even a classroom pet, such as a hamster or fish.

Most rooms have a nice soft carpet, with cozy pillows, tailor made for listening to stories, playing with toys, or hanging out with new friends. There are kid sized desks and tables where children can sit and share the pleasure of having a snack together.

The gear in the room is bursting with hands on activities. There are sand and water tables, art activity centers, marvelous toys, and dazzling books just begging to be read. For the first timer, school shows a lot of promise.

Then we come to grade one. All of a sudden, there aren't so many cool activity centers. Children are pretty excited to have their own desk, but that comes with the caveat that they're expected to sit in it extended periods of time. Except for birthdays and holidays, it isn't likely they will be invited to share a snack or rest on the carpet. It's still an interesting place, but some of the shine has worn off.

Then, with each successive year the classroom becomes less and less stimulating and exhilarating. Yes, some teachers are wonderful at maintaining a motivating and eye-catching space, filled with engaging activities, but the die is cast. Inspiring turns to more Spartan until high school, where most classes have become sterile, no-nonsense learning centers. Could this contribute to some kids getting turned off with school?

You have to ask why we feel just because someone gets older they no longer need interesting surroundings? Think of how dull and un-motivating most of the office spaces in the work world are. Is this the kind of learning and work setting we really want for our kids?

The more businesslike a classroom or a school becomes, the less likely kids will find it a place they enjoy. Creativity becomes more of a challenge, and quantity of education seems to trump exploration and meaningful learning.

There's no practical reason for this to happen. Maybe we just get sloppy. Perhaps we fail to remember classrooms need to inspire, no matter what the level or subject. Your room can be vibrant, exciting and visually eye catching, regardless of the age group. Bring in plants, animals where it's still allowed (the smaller the better). Set up mind motivating activity stations and puzzles. Paint the walls, display students' art throughout the school. Re-arrange the classroom to make it less institutional. Foster dialogue through design, and vice versa.

Yes, it will require some waking up on your part. You'll have to concede that students need stimulation, both by the instructor, and the environment. This will result in extra work on your part, however you probably have twenty or so willing helpers to assist. Invite them be part of the process. The benefits will be huge. Creativity fosters creativity. And if you feel your grade eights still need a sand table for break, so be it!

CHAPTER SIXTEEN

Self Esteem vs. Ego

> Self-praise is for losers. Be a winner. Stand for something. Always have class and be humble.
>
> —John Madden

In one of my many lives, I enjoyed working as an extra in movies and television dramas. Some featured box office stars. Once in a while, we commoners were taken aback when one of the leads came back into the extras' room to have a coffee, bum a smoke or share a funny story. As far as I can see, the reason for the visit was simply to enjoy the company. This self-effacing posture flew in the face of my image of Hollywood celebrities and their egos.

Everyone has ego. It's our sense of self value. Even those with little self-esteem might have an inflated sense of worth. Rampant ego can convince us we're the most precious person in the universe. We believe everything should work for our benefit, all the time. When it doesn't, all of those ugly feelings such as resentment, anger and jealousy rear their heads. Then things get unstable. When our pride strangles us with self-importance, there's little room for anything else, especially compassion. Ego creates an illusion about ourselves. When we're attached to that, there's slim chance of finding the truth about what we really are. The good news is ego has no substance. It's just a construct.

Self-esteem on the other hand, is that magical knowledge we're all right with the universe. We belong where we are, and because we know we're all right, there's no need to put demands on anything or anyone. We can accept what comes along and deal with it the best way we can. When things go wrong we're disappointed, but we're not defeated. We don't lash out and blame others or the world, nor do we resent the success or happiness of others, even in trying circumstances. Self-esteem affords us the luxury of being genuinely concerned for our fellow humans and all living things, with no need to compete with others. Jealousy has no place in our plans.

Living with a healthy self-esteem is a good place to be. Drowning in ego is not. When we're very young, our sense of self is usually nicely balanced. We're fine with who we are, not all puffed up about ourselves. The problem is we get confused as we get older. We see adults who are full of themselves and often mistake this for confidence. Kids often are told they have to look out for number one, and they must protect what they have before someone takes it away. This all gets hammered home through all forms of media. Thinking of yourself first is how you get by.

Now, once you start to think this way, a funny thing happens. Instead of being all powerful and strong, you become fragile and vulnerable. Why is this? Simple; you are always on the defensive, always watching your back. You depend on everything going smoothly and everyone conforming to your ideas in order to be happy. You have everything to lose, and that closes off the natural flow of life.

So even though ego comes dressed up with a lot of whistles and bells, you don't want to be there. Let's try a good self-esteem on for size. Here's how it looks. When you get over your self-importance, you care for others as much as yourself and wish them happiness and well-being. If this sounds a lot like compassion, it's because they go hand in hand. This puts you in a position of power because you don't depend on others or situations for your happiness. Sounds like a good fit?

This runs contrary to what many of us have been told. We're led to believe that being compassionate, caring, and open to others, puts

Self Esteem vs. Ego

us in line to be walked all over. If we let people have an inch they will grab the whole football field. If you've heard this, you can bet our children have too. Not enough children grow up seeing that openness and softness of heart are keys which can unlock all that has real meaning in life.

Through stories or movies of compassion, and through example, we can start turning young people's idea away from the brainwashing they've received from the media and well-meaning adults. We're able to help them understand that the wisdom and power which come from realizing they're tied to others, not in competition. We can incorporate them into language, history lessons, social skills activities and stories of selfless individuals. You can explore the flip side, by examining lives built on egocentricity; lives usually ending in tragedy and non-fulfillment.

Our actions and words have a strong effect on our kids. How we handle ourselves is paramount. Take the time to look at yourself deeply. Imagine you are one of your kids. What are they seeing when they look at you? The message you are sending out may have its impact for years to come. Children have to realize they are fine as they are; that they belong here and they have nothing to prove, or for which to apologize.

No doubt a healthy dose of ego may help us reach certain goals, status or wealth, but it cannot bring happiness or peace to ourselves, or others. The only road which leads there is openness and equanimity, seeing outside of our bubble and exploring the world around us. We can show our kids they can dream and reach their goals, without feeling they will only be measured by their achievements and successes.

CHAPTER SEVENTEEN

For All We Know

> No man can reveal to you aught but that which already lies half asleep in the dawning of your knowledge.
>
> —Kahlil Gibran, *The Prophet*

One of the most unsettling images you can envision, is that of a young boy dressed in battle gear, gun in his hands, ready to defend his country. These children are at an age when most kids in North America are playing baseball. Instead, they are caught in a conflict beyond their control, a war run by adults who believe they hold the moral high ground.

The greatest suffering in his world arises when people accept this kind of deluded reasoning as truth. Ideas become so ingrained into our culture, they are followed through generations without question. We consider it our obligation to hand them over to our children. Apartheid, the Indian Caste system, racial and religious prejudice are just a few of many examples of the wrong beliefs bequeathed to the next generation.

Then there are the subtler, yet still misguided ideas we cling to, like the belief children don't know what life is all about and we, as older and wiser adults need to teach them how to live correctly. It's as if there was something wrong with children that must be fixed, before they grow up.

Stop for just a moment now, close your eyes and recall what it was like to be a child. Remember the innocence and trust you had in the world, how willingly you looked up to the adults in your life. Now with that memory still fresh, open your eyes again and consider the world around you. See how many of the adults carry themselves. Observe the greed, pettiness, exploitation, and cruelty you see not only in the news, but on a personal level. Do you, as that child, find much you aspire to in grownup behaviour? I know this may seem to be a jaded view of life, and there is much that is noble and honourable about the human race. But the fact is much of the lifestyle we urge our children to aim for, is a deception which can never promise fulfilment.

If you take the time to watch your children really carefully, deeply, you'll see that much of the time they have it all worked out. Children are inherently honest, but we teach them to be tactful, coy, and eventually deceitful. They know how to spend their time in mindfulness and living in the moment. As they grow, we teach them idle hands are the devil's hands and equate time with money. Children need very little in life to flourish and be happy. We train them to want things, to need material comforts and possessions, and eventually become avaricious.

It's adults who impart mass consumerism on children not our youth. We lament the fact that kids spend so much time playing video games or glued to their cell phones. We holler when they want a two-hundred-dollar pair of shoes. However, it's adult corporate greed that uses children as one of its most lucrative markets. With constant input, it addicts them to their merchandise and teaches them to consume toxic foods and crave possessions. Never doubt it for a moment, all of this wrong thinking doesn't start with children, it begins with us.

Our children know how to play. They know how to love. They are experts at exploring the wonder of life, and living each moment to its fullest. There's absolutely no reason to suggest they are incomplete, or there is something to fix. Believe it please, children do not need to be fixed.

Unfortunately, it isn't easy to undo such an engrained mind set. What we can do is guide them towards positive choices. We can encourage children to examine life styles more carefully, to take a critical look at the world around them and start to evaluate what works and what doesn't. Before we preach our ideas about what life is, we should be getting their feedback. They must be allowed to voice their opinions with impunity and without fear of derision.

I'm not suggesting our kids don't need our guidance and input, however whether we are a teacher, parent counsellor, coach, or all of these things, we need to be open to a new vision of who children are. They may have much to learn on their journey, and they will acquire a lot of baggage along the way. Let's not pile ours on top of it.

CHAPTER EIGHTEEN

Cultivating the Soil

> It's not what is poured into a student that counts, but what is planted.
>
> —Linda Conway,
> *A Teacher Is Better Than Two Books*

In the days before I moved into a condo and had to give up my garden, I planted tomatoes each spring. I checked around until I found healthy looking seedlings, bought organic black topsoil and mixed it with natural bone meal fertilizer. My babies were gently placed in tidy rows, situated on the sunny side of the yard, and pampered like new born kittens. By doing all this, I gave my tomatoes a pretty good chance of growing up and landing in my salad or BLT. The result of all my nurturing was a good crop of sweet fruit each summer.

For me it was a hobby, but any professional gardener will agree the most important part of growing a garden lies in the preparation. Soil needs to be fortified, turned over and watered in order to increase the odds that your crop will grow up strong and healthy. Sure, you can toss in a bunch of seeds, and with a little luck some may sprout, but without the proper care and cultivation, it's likely you're wasting your time.

While you consider this, contrast it to how we assess and educate our children in their formative years. The system is always in a hurry to ready kids for the future, which on the surface doesn't seem like such a bad thing. But we need to remember there must be a good foundation if we can expect children to blossom. We feed our kids an endless stream of information, and presume this will hold them in good stead for their ride in the adult world. We give them concepts beyond their grasp and expect them to use them later in life. Our academic expectations not only keep expanding, but we insist they be met at younger ages than ever before.

As our standards become more challenging, we lose sight of the purpose of education. The goal is preparation for life, not just for joining the workforce. In our haste to prepare them to compete their way in the modern world, we leave them with little understanding of life, and a very shallow idea of what they are doing and why they are doing it. We continue to up the academic ante, forgetting they are still children and may not be ready to take on the roles we assign them. We might be watering the garden, but it has no rich base in which to flourish, and before long the bloom can definitely go off.

Education is not something to be rushed in order to get our youth out into the adult world. While our kids are young they need a chance to cultivate kindness, openness, curiosity and mindfulness. There has to be time for them to experience, explore and play, without our own motives being forced upon them. Children will only have a sense of peace if they are able to feel the mystery and wonder of life and understand their place in it.

The formative years are the time to give them a head start towards a rewarding life. Overloading them with information and asking them to perform operations they don't fully understand, before they have some sense of self, is like throwing seeds on the ground in the hope they will produce something of substance.

Many adults go through the bulk of their years with the feeling that something is lacking, that all they have achieved is hollow and echoes of emptiness. Ultimately, many start looking for meaning in their later years, when they realize they've missed the mark. The awesome thing is, it's always been, and still is right there in front of their eyes.

Cultivating the Soil

We have the wonderful opportunity to put our kids on the road to living with true meaning. Once started, they have a better chance of remembering all the wonderful things they knew when they were small, before they became buried under the illusions life piles on them. When children are cherished and supported in their self-discovery, their education will have value. We can't assume these things are happening at home. Often, as parents become pressured and stressed, their kids are being left to fend for themselves internally.

Before we get concerned about how much our children can acquire, we should them help appreciate what knowledge can do; how it can give them the opportunity to take what they know, and then open it wide into the world.

History is full of examples of people who have learned how to use their knowledge to make a difference to humanity, and at the same time have a rewarding life. Sharing their stories can have a huge impact and help motivate kids to follow that same path.

Knowledge only has power when it's based on true meaning. It has little significance if it's just handed down information. The early years of education are the time to cultivate our children's curiosity and love of discovery. Then the rest of their schooling has a chance at having some true worth.

CHAPTER NINETEEN

Savouring the Moment

> A poor life this is, if full of care, we have no time to stand and stare?
>
> —William Henry Davis, *No Time to Stare*

> I complete multiplication tables, I draw a butterfly.
>
> —Author's twist on a Zen proverb

Everyone has suffered the dreaded Saturday "to-do" list, the agenda which involves a lot of crossing off until we can finally reclaim our day. In today's world, it seems every day involves a series of tasks to be completed. The grocery shopping is out of the way, the gardening is done, the car is washed, the baby is changed and the kids are off to Karate. Add to that what you do at work and soon everything becomes a chore, something to get out of the way rather enjoyed. Imagine creating a giant list of all the things you had to do until the day you died, and then stroking them off one by one. As you got to the bottom, I guarantee you wouldn't be in such a hurry to get to the last task.

Isn't this what we teach our children? Every day is a succession of jobs that must be completed; the sooner the better. Teachers put up their daily schedules in which each assignment is listed and then checked off. Calendars are ticked off, announcing the demise of each month. You can almost hear the clock as it races to the conclusion of the day, every week and year. Soon we'll be finished with elementary school and go to middle school. When we graduate we can go to high school, and on to college or university and then, the ultimate goal, the job.

Whether we are headed in those directions or not, is irrelevant. It's how we are handling each moment that counts. Sadly, we're rarely encouraged to enjoy the steps along the way. Rather, we're promised that if we make it through them, there will be some kind of payment at the end. But what lies at the end, rather than yet another series of chores? The weekend finally comes, but Monday morning is there before we know it. Then the week stretches out ahead of us again.

While we can't stop the clock, it needn't control us. Of course, we need to have some kind of plan or else nothing will get done, but our plans don't have to become chains. In Buddhist practice, the moment is the essence of life. When you are carrying water, you are just carrying water. You are not thinking of a million other scenarios, or planning tomorrow. There is just the present moment, and from that "now", satisfaction is derived. Look at kids. When they're playing, they are usually fully available to life. They're not arranging their day's activities or berating themselves for not building Lego the day before. Not many children are upset because they played outside in the sun and didn't have time to get to the train set. They are playing and that's enough.

At school, we discourage this kind of presence. Instead, we start to fill children with the sense of urgency of evaluating, planning and completing. All appreciation of the moment is lost in this rush. No wonder so many people end up with a feeling of futility. If we see life as a parade of events, each succeeding the other, what's the point? When do we stop to smell the roses if we're always looking ahead to next year's crop?

TEACHING IN THE SPIRIT

In our quest to teach our lessons and complete assignments, we must never lose sight of the wonder of each second. Nothing is lost when we slow down occasionally and help children rest where they are in any activity, and savour *nowness*. If children are not working solely to finish the job, there's a better chance they will get something out of it along the way. We can be in the moment by simply telling a story, listening to music or looking at a beautiful picture, with no motive except to enjoy.

This doesn't require a complete upheaval of your program. It just calls for a shift in attitude. It is an approach that says several things:

"It's okay if we don't quite finish what we started because we had a great discussion."

"Let's see if we can write a few lines straight from the heart, rather than trying to complete two pages."

"How about taking a few minutes to listen to some music or a favourite story."

"Yes, there's some work to be done, but let's take some time out. We'll take care of it soon enough. Let's linger for a moment."

Maybe, we'll have a signal, such as a small bell, or a handclap, which serves to remind us to stop what we are doing, if only briefly, and come back to the present. Children don't naturally lament the past or feel pressured about the future. We are the ones who turn up the pressure cooker to make them more efficient, more productive. Sometimes, we do it to validate ourselves, so we can say, "Aren't I wonderful, my class did all these things today!" The trouble is, if we're removed from where we are, life is passing us by, leaving nothing in its wake.

There will always be to-do lists in a school day. But if we de-emphasize the need to complete everything and accomplish unreasonable goals, we can make each activity more relaxed and ultimately more meaningful. Then we become available to life, rather than charging through it. At this point life is truly lived, rather than expedited.

CHAPTER TWENTY

Gratitude

> In every thing give thanks.
>
> —1 Thessalonians 5:18

When we took kids away to the outdoor education centre for a few days, the experience of eating in the dining room with friends was a highpoint. Before they stampeded to begin the first of several helpings, I would ask them to stand for just a few moments and think of something for which they were grateful. At first, I helped them out by making suggestions, such as the food they were going to eat, the friends they were with, the beautiful day outside, or even the fact that they were able to get away from their siblings for a few days. At the next meal, they came out with their own, often creative ideas.

As children, many of us were taught to say a few words of thanks at the end of the day, or at the beginning of a meal. A lot of families still uphold this tradition. The problem is, as we get older we may forget the things we have to be thankful for and we certainly don't always give them a loud voice. That noise is reserved for the complaints department. People have a problem that it's Monday, as if they could change it. The weather is always a source of consternation. Perhaps, it's that 8:00 AM appointment. Maybe, they don't like their clothes, their hair, their car, or the coffee they're drinking. If you pay attention to the conversations going on around you, you'll be surprised and maybe sadly amused at the amount of whining and the lack of appreciation.

Children pick up on this very quickly. They hear the grumbling that goes on around them and are fast to follow suit. The moaners attract the largest audience. Not only does this happen in real life but it carries over into the banter they hear over the radio and the shows they watch on TV or online. Since the inception of social media, one only need look at the comments sections to be reminded how far removed we are from recognizing what an amazing gift life is. In short, it appears negativity tops gratitude.

In a busy, plugged in world, you don't run across much that encourages children to take stock of what they have and express their thanks for it. This becomes a pattern, an attitude that life owes us something and often comes up short of our expectations. When we're busy thinking we've been cheated in life, it's very difficult to take a lot of joy in what we have. This carries over to the way we view others. We often end up being suspicious of others, rather than seeing the good in them.

Here's where you come in. Are you aware your own life is a totally awesome miracle? If not, check out Ali Binazir's *What Are the Odds?* or Stephen Hawking's *Life in The Universe*. Once you're on board with that, you are better equipped to help guide children into a mind-set of looking at what they have, as opposed to what's missing. Of course, some children have every reason in the world to feel down on life, maybe because of their home situation, physical disabilities or the baggage they are carrying. These kids need extra help in nurturing a more positive outlook of the world, and finding the things that are right with their lives, but remember, challenges are what you do best.

Try starting each day with your students, preferably sitting in a circle, where there's more sense of community, and take a few moments to talk about the things we all have be grateful for. This can make a total difference in the way everyone approaches the day ahead. Remember, most kids, not unlike yourself, rise in a hurry, rush to get ready for school, and dash out the door in order to be on time. By plunging straight into school work, there's no time at all to ease into the day and become okay with it.

Gratitude

At first, children may have difficulty deciding what it is they appreciate, but with guidance, the list will become limitless. How about we start with their health, a warm home, place to sleep, food to eat and someone who cares for them and loves them? For most kids, these will be a given, but a little reminder doesn't hurt. Then if you give them time, they will expand on that. It may be material, such as that lucrative trip to Toys R Us on the weekend. Or it may be global, being thankful they live in a place where they are basically safe on the street, where there is no war around them. Try to get all the kids to participate, even if they have to repeat what's already been said. Encourage them to think from the heart, and share it with the class. As a spring board, read some stories about children who have risen above their personal challenges.

From time to time you may be asked who we are thanking. Don't sweat the question. Just tell them that it doesn't much matter. Explain how some may say thanks to God, while others will thank their parents. Perhaps, we can recognize the Universe or the Earth for providing what we have. The point is, we are becoming aware of the things for which we are grateful, and expressing them. There is a tremendous power generated when gratitude is sincerely conveyed.

For children with hard home lives, much of what they express may revolve around school, as this may be their refuge. When I worked with kids with challenging lives, it was hard for them to see the good side of anything. I had to keep badgering them, reminding them about what they did have and what was good about the day. I was careful not to trivialize their disappointments, but I would try to encourage them to see the other side of their lives, the side which had promise.

Communicating appreciation is not a one-shot deal, to be exercised when you have a few free moments, but rather, it needs to be an integral part of the day, starting first thing in the morning. Even children who are having what they call "a bad day" can find their outlook spinning off in a whole new direction when this time is shared in such a meaningful way.

You might decide to have the children keep some kind of informal thankfulness journal, which could include the offerings made by staff and students. Classes can exchange their ideas with other members of the school population. You might create murals and posters to decorate the school. How about having children reading their own feelings of appreciation to the school during morning announcements? Gratitude contagion is a wonderful thing.

In the Tribes program, activities are never considered complete until there has been a brief acknowledgment of appreciation for fellow participants. This demonstration of gratitude is an ideal way to finish the school day. After agenda checks and clean-up, have the kids re-assemble in the circle and briefly offer their thanks to another classmate, or give their appreciation for some activity that occurred during the day. Once the ball starts rolling it will flow easily. As teachers, you may have to offer some guidance, as kids will tend to offer compliments to their friends, or the most popular child in the class. With a little help on your part, they will be able to spread their thankfulness so everyone feels included. Don't forget to give your own personal words to your class.

Please, don't let the bustle and pressure of the day's activities push these moments to the side. They are as valuable as any other time you'll spend during the day. If this is started in the earliest grades and pursued throughout a child's schooling, children can develop a new way of looking at the world, which can only make their lives richer.

CHAPTER TWENTY-ONE

A Moment of Peace

> When you find peace within yourself, you can become the kind of person who can live at peace with others.
>
> —Peace Pilgrim

Step into any school close to Remembrance Day, and you are almost certain to see kids busily preparing banners and poems. They may be writing a personal vision about what peace means to them, or perhaps, an original story. Some of their ideas will be surprisingly insightful, with a wide range of meanings, similes and metaphors. Others may be simple, but one thing is certain, they all contain hope and yearning for a peaceful world.

This is no surprise, when you consider the world can be a scary place, where kids are constantly bombarded with news of violent acts and war. It's right in front of them on the TV every day. Remember, bad news sells, and the media dishes out what the public wants to see. Then we hand our kids the challenge that it's this generation which has the power and the duty to make a difference, to clean up the mess we're handing them. Interesting point of view.

Knowing this, ask yourself what we do to promote and further peace throughout the year in our schools. How can we be sure our children don't reach adulthood accepting or expecting violence and

TEACHING IN THE SPIRIT

terror to be the norm? Instead, is it possible for them to grow up not only hoping, but knowing peace can be achieved?

Every November 11th, when we set aside time to pray for peace and remember the horrors of war, there are those who suggest we are glorifying warfare. However, when you look deeply, you realize the support we show is for our veterans. When we honour those who have fallen, we are bringing to light the human spirit. The departed are part of who we are today and recognizing and respecting them is one way to create a solid foundation upon which peace can be built.

The search for peace is not a one-off, to be discarded on November 12th, any more than caring and giving is confined to December 25th. It must be woven into the fabric of each day. The power unleashed when people have a common goal, is immense. Think how much strength would be created if we took time each day to turn our thoughts to the prospect of world peace. On top of that, by contemplating peace as a regular part of our lives, we give our kids a mindset it can and will be attained, and we can all be an important part of the process.

You don't need a lesson plan for this. It can be part of the morning routine. A minute for peace could be observed by the school on a regular basis, possibly followed by some open dialogue in class. Children might be asked what they feel when they stand silently on Remembrance Day. What does peace look like or feel like? How do you envision a peaceful world? Describe some peace actions. What kinds of acts are not peaceful actions? The talk can range from local and school activities, to larger scale connections.

This is a wonderful state of mind in which to start a school day and can also be the motivation for many other writing, drama, art, and music activities. Think of the striking message visitors would receive when they entered a school decorated in posters and artwork depicting loving and peaceful ideas and scenes.

So many hours of a child's life are spent in school. It seems to be a kindness to them, and an acknowledgment of the role they will play, to spend a few minutes each day considering ways in which a more optimistic, harmonious and secure outlook for the future can be generated. Children have spent so much of their lives being frightened by what others have told them, they often take it to heart.

A Moment of Peace

This can build up in their store consciousness. In time it all gets too heavy and can surface in a gloomy outlook towards life.

Long before this takes hold, we can begin to ease the negativity being planted in children's minds and assure them they can make a positive change. When they start to feel more at peace with themselves, it will spread to those around them. This is where global peace starts, not in the offices of the world's leaders. We all have to realize peace is not a revolution. It is born out of the smallest of actions and thoughts, and from there it grows and thrives until a new world is possible.

CHAPTER TWENTY-TWO

Compassion 101

> When you feel someone else's suffering, there is a birth of understanding.
>
> —Deepak Chopra, *Peace is the Way*

During the first Iraq war, a young Japanese girl felt the call to go and help those citizens who were suffering from the long and devastating conflict. After she returned to her native Japan, she was shunned by her former co-workers and friends. Her family received death threats. Why was this? Clearly it was because to her critics, she had shown compassion to the wrong side. For those who were too blind to see, softness of heart was something we only show to those with whom we agree. But for this caring young woman, suffering was universal. There were no sides to pick, because compassion takes no sides and makes no judgments.

Compassion is a quality that lies within all of us. What is compassion? Loosely defined, it's no more than genuinely wishing the best for all living beings. Notice there are no disclaimers here. Now, even the hardest heart will experience a twinge of sadness when it sees intense suffering in fellow humans or animals. However, for many of us, compassion lies buried beneath the layers the years have accrued. At best, with many people it's selective. We feel it for our children when they hurt. We have flashes when we hear a moving story or see a sentimental film. But is it something which guides our lives in everything we say or do? This is where many of us fail. Sometimes we're too wound up in our own daily dramas to truly look around us, and see the world. We may sympathize with the victims in our society, but it is much harder to feel anything but disdain for perpetrators of crime and violence. Yet if there is to be true change, we must be able to feel compassion for all, for the Earth herself. Healing starts within each of us.

The seeds are there all right, but we need a good shaking to stir them into life, to remember we're all one, and that the slightest suffering affects the whole. When compassion is re-awakened, we begin to live it in everything we do. Our hearts don't just go out to our loved ones, but everyone, without discrimination. For this to happen, we first need to be gentle and forgiving to ourselves.

We cannot suppose this is what children are learning at home. Even children in a loving, nurturing environment may not be able to see beyond their own lives. If that foundation isn't being laid at the family level, it's our opportunity to present these values at school.

Infants live in a rather narrow world. It is largely restricted to ensuring their needs are meet. However, once their world begins to expand to include a wider number of people, we can help awaken sleeping compassion. Early pre-school and kindergarten emphasize the value of sharing, helping, and caring for each other, but in many cases as children grow older, these values are not particularly nurtured or expanded in scope. These attitudes have to be fostered at all levels, not just the once a month character trait which has become the trend. They need to be woven into every aspect of learning and life.

In the classroom, when we're teaching the physical and economic geography of the world, we need to put aside our exclusive study of profits and economic growth, and focus on our responsibility and commitment to the welfare of all. In the end, this is what really matters. Teaching history is largely based on memorizing facts and analyzing the causes and effects of events. However, we can look more deeply into our past, putting ourselves in the place of those we are studying. We don't have to change our areas of study, just our viewpoint, looking at a larger picture, shifting the way we see the world. Then we can become much less clinical and awaken our children's awareness and openness towards each situation. We might start by examining international conflicts and looking at alternative actions, where restraint might have been used.

As with all teaching, the best place to start is with what is familiar. Some schools already have programs where students provide service to younger children or senior citizens. Most community services are crying out for volunteers. What a bonus for them to have young willing helpers, and what a wonderful lesson in community and caring this provides for children. Remember, most children are not so much indifferent, as they are unaware of the needs of others.

When I taught grade eight social studies I included a unit in which the kids would research various humanitarian efforts on the Internet. They would look up the sites of organizations such as War Child, UNICEF, Green Peace and Free the Children. After exploring the efforts of these groups to heal the planet and alleviate suffering, they would share and invite their peers to express their feelings. Judging by some of the questions asked and the discussions which followed, I know this exercise helped to open a few eyes and expand some minds.

Even if they are familiar with the names, most children know little about these establishments and they have no idea of the huge numbers of people who dedicate their lives to helping others. Names like Albert Sweitzer and Jimmy Carter are completely foreign to most teaching agendas. By taking a deeper look into the outward manifestations of compassion, children start to have a less self-centered view of the world.

At one of my former schools our student council adopted a foster child overseas. The small monthly payment was obtained through various fund-raising schemes that the children loved. The kids always knew the dance they looked forward to, was going to help another child somewhere in the world, a child who had the misfortune to be in a very different set circumstances than themselves. When a letter or communication arrived, it was put into the display case, and copies of the letter were "mailed" to each classroom. There, the students were kept updated about their brother's

Compassion 101

or sister's progress. They wrote letters or poems and drew pictures to be sent to their foster child. Students explored their foster child's home country and lifestyle. It was a wonderful opportunity for children to be reminded of the many things for which they could be thankful.

More recently the "Free the Children" initiative founded by Craig Keilburger has been embraced by many schools. This supports children throughout the world and opens an awareness and sense of connection in our kids which may carry on throughout their entire lives.

When children are informed, then compassion and kindness begin to flourish once again. Too often children hear it's a dog eat dog world out there and you have to look out for number one. By teaching true caring and softness of heart, children awaken not only to the suffering of others, but they are easier on themselves. They do look out for themselves, but instead of it being at the expense of others, it is with an all-encompassing compassion, one which has the welfare of all at its heart.

CHAPTER TWENTY-THREE

Leading to Truth

> The greater the force of your altruistic attitude toward sentient beings, the more courageous you become.
>
> —The Dalai Lama

A Buddhist legend tells of a fearsome warrior who spent his life conquering and pillaging kingdoms and monasteries. In one such hermitage, he had little trouble breaking through the gates and massacring many of the monks. At the height of the rout an old holy man jumped out in front of his horse.

The warrior angrily shouted, "Old man, do you know who I am? Do you know that I can run you through with my sword and not give it a second thought?"

Calmly the monk replied, "Brave knight, do you know who I am? I can let you can run me through with your sword and not give it a second thought."

According to the story, the soldier was so awed with this show of true power, he laid down his sword and vowed to follow the master.

By the time they enter the school system our children have already started to accept a lot of false ideas. These same illusions are constantly re-enforced everyday by the media, the written word, role models and peers.

One huge illusion involves the concept of power. There are different ways in which we define power. Militarily, power equals superior strength and arsenals. The United States is touted as the world's greatest super power. Emerging nations with new weapons are a threat because they now have the potential for destruction. The economy is another measure of power.

In the video games children play and the movies they watch, power is always identified with physical strength, superior fighting ability and strategy, and the cache of weapons possessed by each side.

On the business and financial front, power comes from money. The more wealth you have, the more people you can control and so you have clout. Still others tell us time is power, or perhaps knowledge is. Learning to become a strong negotiator and will help you to gain control. Power can be something we acquire if we fight for it, or we happen to find ourselves in the right set of circumstances.

Children can become easily duped into believing they will have strength if they attain enough money, muscle or knowledge. If this notion persists, they may continue to strive for it throughout their adult lives, but try as they may, they will never find true power.

True power is much more than all the things we're told, and kids need to learn it early. Authentic strength comes from inside. It springs from holding to what you know is true, no matter what life brings. It dwells in responding to everything with compassion. Power comes from the way we hold ourselves in a calm and centered manner. It's a quiet confidence that we are right with the world. We make no apologies for who we are, and have no need to flaunt whatever form of authority we have. Despite all the myths and lies, when we meet someone with true power, we immediately feel it because it surrounds their very being, and we're enveloped by it. Gandhi had power. Martin Luther King had power. Everything in the life of Nelson Mandela exuded power.

As children grow, we need to help them identify true strength by tearing down the lies, because what they've been told is power, is nothing more than brute force or intolerance, often driven by greed or ego. Children need to recognize that this will never bring them actual power, and never improve their own lives or the lives of anyone else.

This is where we come in. Start by familiarizing children with individuals who have shown truth in the way they lived. People whose every action and word illustrate the real meaning of power. Share their stories and discuss what qualities led these individuals to make such an impact on the world. Have children suggest how they can bring true acts of power into their own lives. Assure them they don't have to run out and save the world and become heroes. By being true to what they know and acting in a selfless, courageous and loving manner, they are growing in their own stature. By opening and softening their hearts even in the most difficult circumstances, they are more powerful than the strongest army or richest tycoon. Then they can become a force for positive change.

Every day, re-enforce positive actions in the classroom. Let children identify with role models who are symbols of mastery. Banish forever the idea that by acting in a loving, caring, and compassionate manner to others, you are giving away anything. Show them how every kind act, word or action delivered from the heart, affects the whole. They may then be less likely to spend their lives pursuing a mirage, and start to feel and use the wealth already in their hands.

CHAPTER TWENTY-FOUR

Visualization

> What if you slept?
> And what if in your sleep you dreamed?
> And what if in your dream, you went to heaven
> And there plucked a strange and beautiful flower.
> And what if when you awoke
> You had the flower in your hand?
>
> —Samuel Taylor Coleridge,
> *What If You Slept?*

I love to read *Calvin and Hobbes*. To me, what makes Calvin so special is his flair for day dreaming. A single word from his teacher sends him spinning light years into the universe, to become the hero of the galaxy. He gets through his suppertime vegetables by picturing them to be foul smelling creatures which must be conquered. His report card may be peppered with D's but his imagination is fertile. If we could put Calvin 20 years into the future we might find him creating new video games, or writing graphic novels which kids would fight over in the school library.

What many like to dismiss as daydreaming, I would rather call inspired visualization. Children spend much of their time in the world of make believe. Many of the games they play, especially on their own, involve using their creativity to fill in the missing pieces. They may have a plastic sword to play with, but it's that touch of whimsy which turns the couch into a castle, and assembles it with knights and damsels.

Parents may laud this kind of creativity when their child is very young. However, when kids approach school age, this inspiration is called daydreaming and must abandoned with childhood. At school, kids are kept so busy there's little time to engage in this kind of reverie, and if they indulge in the habit, they're certain to be embarrassed as they are called upon to repeat what their teacher just said.

If that isn't enough to scare away inspiration, the electronically-generated stimuli which forever envelops our kids has taken away much of their ability to day dream. Problems are resolved during a 60-minute television show; the dragon's quest is now completed through the various levels of the latest video game, and if that doesn't do the trick, there are cheats to help ensure victory. Children are so busy receiving input that their ability to generate their own inventions has been seriously impaired. What is there to imagine when you can have the virtual world of your choosing at the push of a button?

So let's go back and look at what Lama Surya Das calls Conscious Drifting. This ability to imagine and manifest has resulted in the biggest strides and important inventions throughout history. Those people whose lives we consider great, all had one thing in common; an ability to see beyond what their eyes and ears told them, a capacity to turn fantasy into reality. The idea of air travel, space flight, mobile phones and skyping would once have been considered ridiculous, but those things are now so common place we don't give them a second thought. Imagine handing Plato a cell phone as you put him aboard his Trans-Atlantic flight. He would pinch himself to see if it was real. Everything created by humans stems from our ideas, not from materials. Sadly, this gift of creativity, isn't fostered by our cerebral approach to learning, which is centered on quantification and empiricism.

If our kids are going to have any chance at all to rise beyond the ordinary and break from the matrix we have created, then they must re-gain their ability to visualize. Parents need to turn off the TV,

Visualization

restrict the hours spent in front of video games, and help kids recapture the wonder of imaginative playtime. As parents, we should be happy to see our children playing creative games with other children, rather than being glued in isolation to a screen.

As teachers, we can give kids time to daydream each day. Take a short period when your students can put their heads down and close their eyes, listen to some soothing music and drift wherever their mind takes them. Have a few moments where there is no activity, no formal learning, no one talking; just a chance to let awareness expand. Shake things up by asking them to write down or express verbally what they think certain sounds look like, or what different objects sound like. Fancy hearing the flowers sing, or seeing the wind when it is howling. As their leader, you need to move outside your comfort zone and foster the incredible.

Another exercise is for the teacher to generate a story or a scenario for children to imagine while they are listening quietly. You could invite them to picture lying in a grassy field on a warm summer day, feeling the breeze blowing, smelling the flowers. Construct a mental stage and then have them generate their own story, one child, a line at a time.

We're way beyond the old idea of giving kids a topic and expecting them to write a story in a half an hour. That means you need to become an active participant, not just a supervisor. When we give a child a chance to imagine once again, we start the brain reconnecting circuits which have been severely neglected over the years. Once we start exercising this part of the mind, we rekindle the wonder of life, the belief in possibilities. Our kids can break away from the ordinary and the only natural step from there, is to move into the extraordinary.

CHAPTER TWENTY-FIVE

Don't Just Do Something, Sit There

> The dove doesn't know if she'll eat tonight, but she's singing anyway.
>
> —Rumi

Do you know someone who is incapable of being still and doing nothing? He's a whirlwind of activity, constantly running, on the go. Any down time must be filled. When there's silence, it gets contaminated with talk. His entire life is abuzz with busyness. The TV is going in the background, the radio is blaring, or he's constantly checking his phone. Just watching him makes you weary.

People like this are products of our activity-crazed society and they're not small in numbers. How many people do you know who are comfortable without any goal or activity, who can just walk when they are walking, or sit and enjoy silence? Not a lot I'd bet.

In particular, North American society doesn't take inactivity lightly. Idle hands are the devil's hands, was the creed of our ancestors, when leisure was equated with sloth. It's a belief which still seems to run in our genes. It's as if we must always be constructively engaged for our time to have meaning. So we gallop through our days, as if running a race, too occupied to take a time out. Breaks are usually on the run, while we check the clock. Weekends are congested with trips to box stores, spring cleaning, repairs and taking the kids to their various activities. If we don't have a list of chores, we invent things to do.

It's ironic how we poke fun of people who value leisure time. We're far too important and busy to have a rest during the day, as is tradition in some of the more grounded cultures. We don't have time to savour a leisurely lunch, enjoy a siesta or take time with our families. Our preoccupation with work and achievement is slowly eroding even these traditions. Many workers stuff down a sandwich while sitting at their desks. All of this busyness borders on the manic. Technology, rather than creating more leisure, has made us more obsessed with activity than ever. When we're away from the office, our pagers, phones and emails keep the chain linked.

If that's not bad enough, we pass this mania on to our children. The whole school day becomes a deadline. Language must occupy a certain percentage of the morning. Math has to follow. After that we try to cram in Science, Social Studies, the Arts and Gym. Voluminous expectations must be taught, tested and evaluated. Birthday parties, games and bonding time with peers are considered wasted, and waste is taboo. With this frenzied pace there is little time to actually enjoy what we're doing. Yes, I did say enjoy.

Now, let me assure you I'm not suggesting for a moment that we spend our school days lolling about on the carpet, eating chocolates. Completing a meaningful task is a rewarding experience. Students rise to challenges and would be bored to tears without them. On top of that, they would learn little and be ill prepared for the life which lies ahead.

So how do we make it all work? That magic word balance comes up again. There are things we want to get done, expectations to meet, and dreaded deadlines; but the key is to blend it with a sense of play. Create an aura of relaxation around the work we do. Work hard at times, but don't be afraid to have some down time. Have an occasional "lazy afternoon," and spend some time daydreaming, playing board games, sitting in circle and just talking, getting to know more about each other. Keep away from the computer and movies. This is real decompression time. Help kids appreciate that every waking moment need not be filled with activity and sometimes it's okay to just chill for a while.

After a holiday or even a weekend, get back into the routine gently and gradually. Don't expect kids to always go from zero to 60 in the first 10 minutes. Show your kids by example, you too can take off your shoes and unwind, and that even adults don't need to be dashing about every moment of the day. In time, you'll find your own fit for your style. Although some may question your motives, as educators you know the reality of teaching better than anyone. Spread the message that more is not necessarily better.

Our expectations are now so vast that teachers have little time for anything else. Those who keep increasing the demands on instructors and students are unaware of how impractical they've become. Perhaps some time back in the classroom would foster perspective. Classroom teachers should be more involved in programming from the top, because they are the only ones who fully understand the damage unreasonable objectives have on our schools. The media, who cry for higher standards, need to do their homework and spend some time in the field, before getting on their high horses and condemning our efforts. When we work in a frenzied atmosphere we all lose.

When we relax about education, we can combine a creative, productive classroom with an unhurried, non-pressured atmosphere. As our students grow into adults they will be equally gratified tackling a challenging project, or simply letting go and just being. The beauty is, they'll do it without guilt, because there's nothing to prove now they are able to balance work and play.

CHAPTER TWENTY-SIX

Getting the Connection

> Never give children the chance to believe that
> anything exists in isolation. Make it plain from the
> start that all of life is relationship.
>
> —Aldous Huxley, *The Island*

A 1950's sci-fi movie poster, warns "WE ARE NOT ALONE!" While the message was intended to scare, I believe it should be hung from the rafters all over civilization. Think about it. WE ARE NOT ALONE! Even if we are the only inhabited planet in the universe, or we live in the wilds of the Yukon and it feels we haven't a friend, we are never alone.

Sadly, many of us spend much of our lives feeling isolated and abandoned. Despite the love of family and friends, many of us frequently experience a disconnect with the flow of life. Most Eastern philosophy recognizes that a major cause of this form of suffering occurs when our egos rip us away from the flow of life. Often, we see ourselves struggling against a cruel and impersonal cosmos. While technology may bring us a thousand friends on Facebook, it severs us from personal intimacy, and gives us no lasting satisfaction. The good news is, this concept of loneliness is self-created and anything we can make, we can dismantle.

TEACHING IN THE SPIRIT

When we are immersed in ourselves, we imagine we are the centre of the universe, solitary warriors fighting the world, relating to little more than our immediate family and circle of friends. Life is taken for granted, with little time spent appreciating what we have, or being happy to just be alive. The effect of this is the pervading sense of separation and futility, that *What's it all for?* mind set.

The plain truth is, we are not isolated beings, struggling to survive. We are part of what the ancients Buddhists called Indra's Net. This Sanskrit phrase is a metaphor for the connection of everything in existence. The elements which comprise the universe are the same ones which run through our bodies. The mind we experience and cherish so deeply, which also causes us grief, is just a drop in the ocean of consciousness. Nothing we ever do, say or feel is a separate action. Only our sense of self gives us this illusion.

The challenge lies in moving from understanding this, to knowing it in our hearts and then living it daily. It's possible to re-awaken this knowledge, and as we do, we can break away from the raft of division into the sea of unity. There are countless ways to help our children remember this. With simple reminders and practice, we can stop the ego from doing its splitting act and allow kids to see the world as it really is.

Have the kids pick up a piece of paper. Ask them where it comes from. They might be able to venture that it came from a tree. That's a good start. But where did the tree come from? The tree came from the forest. How did the forest come to be? There was Earth, and the Sun and the rain fell on the ground and the tree grew. The rain came from the clouds, which came from the water on the land and in the oceans. That same tree was cut by a lumberjack who had a mother and a father like you. He drove a truck which was made by men and women who also had mothers and fathers. They ate food made by farmers in fields, very much like the ground in which the trees grew, the same trees which made the paper you now hold. When this paper has been used it will be recycled and made into other products by men and women who have families with children very much like yourself. Someday, another child in another city, will hold the transformed paper you now hold in your hands and use it, perhaps as a drinking cup or a ticket to a hockey game. So when you hold a piece of paper, you are holding the sun, the rain, the soil, all the other components which helped create it. That's a pretty awesome concept.

Draw this web on chart paper or Smartboard and invite a student to remove some pieces to see what happens. This is great fun and can be played over and over, using different items. In the process of making connections, something wonderful happens. Children start to see nothing really exists on its own. Rather, it's just one piece in an unimaginably endless puzzle.

This thinking, called *inter-isness* by Buddhist master Thich Naht Hanh, helps us overcome the sense of self-importance which leaves us feeling deserted and rejected. Recalling connection brings us back to feeling our inter-existence with the whole of life and being. We can remind children to be thankful to everyone and everything, because it is the kindness and grace of others that give us all what we have. This takes nothing from individuality, but illustrates how we are so much more than just that. When we think this way nothing of ourselves is lost, and everything is gained.

You can draw wonderful murals and art pieces, showing this inter-existence. Give the kids a simple item and see how far they can expand it. Have an oral exercise in the morning using the foods they had for breakfast. Soon it will become second nature to think beyond the obvious. A major step in returning to full consciousness in daily living, is restoring the wonder and awareness of the ordinary.

By living in fuller mindfulness of the way things really exist, our children will be spared much of the desperation and hopelessness which pervades this world, and instead feel a sense of connection. That isn't a fairy tale or religion, it's plain science.

CHAPTER TWENTY-SEVEN

The Joy of Walking

> The trail is beautiful. Be still.
>
> —anonymous Dakota saying

I love to walk, be it summer, the dead of winter or those spaces in between. I walk in the rain and the snow. Each time of year has its own unique beauty. Walking helps me forget myself, because when I am out hiking I'm generally not doing anything else. It's a time when I can enjoy each footstep, leave my stories behind, and settle. Whether it's a gentle stroll or a faster pace, it refreshes, rejuvenates and energizes. Anyone who walks knows when you're finished, no matter how agitated you were when you started, everything seems to be a clearer, and life, more spacious. Walking is great therapy for anyone experiencing stress.

We see people out strolling in parks on Sunday afternoon. Folks are out early in the morning and late at night with their dogs. Suits amble around public squares downtown during their lunch break. Somewhere inside, we know how joyful and therapeutic walking can be.

So the logical question is, "Why don't we spend more time outside with kids, introducing them to one of the most basic yet rewarding pleasures life can offer? It's a way of counteracting our kid's sedentary life style. No one can argue the benefits of taking children out into nature. So now we've established that, let's start walking.

Before we set off, let's be clear. We're not on a journey to get anywhere. Nor are we carrying a clipboard to answer questions. We're walking for its own sake, because it's fun.

Yes, I've said the "f" word. It seems when we take a trip out of the school, fun isn't always a part of the agenda, and you must have a dozen curriculum related justifications to get approval to go. But sometimes, in our quest to find meaning, we miss the most accessible and worthwhile opportunities. I'm saying the simple act of getting out and walking is more than enough rationale for leaving the school. Aside from the exercise, we're giving the kids a chance to step back from their work and routine. We're also connecting with our neighbourhood.

Now, what do we do on our little stroll? That's the fun part. We do nothing. We just walk and see where it leads us. Maybe we'll go to a field or park where we can all just stretch out on the grass and look at the sky. With primary kids, we might imagine clouds turning into animals. Or maybe we have the time to sit beside a running brook and listen to the babbling water. With luck, we'll see some of the local wildlife, possibly feed the birds or squirrels.

How about sketching nature? The beautiful thing is it doesn't much matter what we do, because we didn't really set out to accomplish anything in the first place. You aren't really lost if you don't have a destination.

Getting our kids outside just for its own sake is the ideal situation, but if it won't fly with the big boss, then the next best thing is to take them outside for a reason. It doesn't take a lot of creativity to tie your walk in with the curriculum, if you must. In a natural setting you connect with life studies, habitats and natural ecosystems. If your area is more built up, you can find links to local history, geography or community studies. Motion and physical activity will hook you up with Health Sciences and Phys. Ed. Now that you're thinking creatively, just imagine how you can tie this in with the Arts, Language and even Math. Once your thinking becomes more open, you'll have no trouble creating goals. If you have a more enlightened leader, you likely won't have to go through this fuss.

TEACHING IN THE SPIRIT

In walking, we teach children there is beauty to be found in the ordinary, and it is accessible any time we wish. Whether it's walking, staring at the stars, or whacking golf balls at the driving range, anything which disengages the mind opens us to endless possibilities.

All of their lives, children are going to be told activities must have meaning, an end goal. Meanwhile the days slip by in a whirl of busyness. When kids first enter school, it's the perfect time to baptize them into the joys of walking.

For some of us lucky enough to have an open area nearby, we simply need to get an ongoing permission form to take the kids walking. Even a half an hour can do wonders. So if your school is near an open area, why haven't you done this yet?

If you're in an inner-city area, you can walk around the block. Why not hop a local bus and go to the closest wildlife area? Even the sounds of the city can be part of conscious drifting. We ask kids for money for other educational excursions. Why not bus fare to get to a park or natural setting?

If we get out kids walking when they are young, it will become a part of their life as they grow older.

As their leader, you can keep your eyes and ears open for things to explore along the way. There may be butterflies on the flowers. Raindrops may be glistening on a spider web. A cicada may be singing in the trees. Maybe, the sounds will be exciting, such as fire engine sirens or road drills. In the end, it's all the same. Let the kids take some time to watch, listen and absorb the everyday wonders around them.

Maybe, you will sing in rhythm to your steps, like desert nomads. Perhaps, your walk will be silent. However, you plan it, you're helping your children expand their awareness and open their minds, away from all the limits of life. If this isn't justification for a trip, then none exists.

CHAPTER TWENTY-EIGHT

The Myth of Good and Bad

> A single leaf cannot turn yellow, without the knowledge of the whole tree.
>
> —Kahlil Gibran, *The Prophet*

I swear my Grade 8 Health teacher enjoyed scaring us by listing all the horrible diseases we could contract and which foods were toxic. His extensive list included caffeine. Since his word was the gospel, I rushed home and told my mother she shouldn't be drinking tea, as no good would come of it. Being from a good British household, this didn't impress her much. However, she took the time to explain that yes, having too much caffeine was not healthy, but tea and coffee were not necessarily bad things in themselves. She was introducing me to the concept of balance.

Later, my own homeroom students would come to me from health class with homemade posters proclaiming the evils of snacking, wine, sex, smoking, and drugs. While we know teaching healthy life choices is essential to educating our youth, we must be mindful not to pigeonhole everything as good or bad, because there usually is more to the story.

From the time we were babies we were told fairy tales about evil witches and good princes. We are warned of bad people who try to hurt young children. When we watch the current events of the day, we make judgments. Choices are either right or wrong. Duality is ingrained in children at a very young age and is re-enforced throughout their childhood years, both in and out of school. As we soon discover however, things are not often so clear. There's a lot of space between the poles, although some are never able to see it that way.

There are simple ways we can help kids realize that everything is not cut and dry. We can try reading traditional stories and fairy tales to the children, and ask them to view the other side of the story as they listen. How does the giant feel in *Jack and the Beanstalk?* Why do you think the step sisters are so mean to Cinderella? Maybe, the Troll has reasons for being angry with the three Billy Goats. Perhaps, he's sick and tired of them thumping up and down on his bridge when he's trying to sleep. This exercise is fun for kids, and it also helps them to start looking at situations from all sides. It can be expanded into drama activities. You'll be surprised at how many will now want to play the villain's role.

When we teach kids, it goes with the territory that we're helping them to look at the world and make decisions which will make for a happier and healthier life. But we need to be sure our young people don't grow up seeing everything as simply being right or wrong. The trap of constantly finding ourselves in judgment of people and events taints our way of looking at the world. If we're mired in judgment we start to lose sight of who we are, because self takes over and makes us feel puffed up and superior to others. We then become preoccupied with evaluating the decisions and choices of others, paving the road for a fear based outlook on the world. Take a look at the local rag newspaper, the one that always has headlines constantly expressing outrage, usually wanting to hang anyone who breaks the law. Sadly, there are a lot of people who think that way. The notion we always need to take sides can lead us down the path to bigotry and intolerance if we're not careful.

All we have to do is make a subtle shift in the way we present information to children, in order to open their minds. Sometimes there is no grey. If a child is about to run into traffic, we don't analyze the situation. Sharp action is definitely in order. However, as children become old enough to filter the input they receive, it's important to avoid always classifying things into rigid classes. Instead, steer them towards examining events and choices in terms of what really works in this world. When seeing current affairs unfold, we can widen our children's outlook by encouraging them to consider all possible sides of the story, to start viewing each event with compassion and understanding. Even when events have a critical or personal impact, look at them from a standpoint of openness rather than from some preconceived or programmed notion.

As our kids get older, we can encourage open, frank, and honest examination of the world, the insight to see there are many angles to view situations, and when they shift their perspective shifts ever so slightly, they just may see things which were not visible before. We can assure them it's fine to be astute in their positions, but that doesn't have to always involve making blanket condemnations of the alternatives.

Once we have helped children let go of rigid labels, they are less likely to become caught up in this myth of good and bad. They will become acutely aware of their options and decisions, ones which come from having looked at things from a position of openness and understanding, rather than bias or fear. At this point, their minds become infinitely vaster and filled with possibilities, and they start to see the world and others with compassion and equanimity.

CHAPTER TWENTY-NINE

Walking in Beauty

> When this Holy Man went off into the woods, he knew everything he knew, more than you or I, without teachers, without books, just because he believed in the river.
>
> —Herman Hesse, *Siddhartha*

In his autobiography, *The Wind Is My Mother*, Bear Heart shares the story about his mother taking him out to the hilltop not far from his home, at the age of three. There in the native tradition, she introduced Bear Heart to the four directions; East, South, West and North. She made a blessing to each, so they would protect him and bring balance into his life.

    She presented the sun to him and prayed its warmth would surround him with her life-giving energy. The wind was invoked to bless him, and so he in turn, would always cherish the wind and know its value to the Earth. She showed him the water and exalted its presence, which enables living things to survive on this planet. He was then anointed with ashes and received the consecration of fire.

Walking in Beauty

When the sun had gone down, the moon and the stars revealed themselves, along with their place in the order of the universe and their radiant light which shines through the darkness.

Bear Heart says as he grew up, he felt a profound sense of balance and belonging because of the relationship his people had with nature. He learned to cherish and respect the universal elements, neither looking down upon, or up to nature, but being at one with it.

Not many children come close to receiving this amazing gift. Most are lucky to get the occasional camping trip or picnic in the country. Some kids reach High School without ever moving outside the concrete walls of the city. You can extol the virtues of the city all you like, but if you are not able to spend time with nature, you're losing a huge part of your life. Despite this, I do love living in the city. The sounds of music, the wonderful tastes and smells in the restaurants; the entertainment and the sports are stimulating to the senses. But I also feel lucky to live five minutes from walking trails, forests and a river. One hour walking in those surroundings and the world seems a lot more comfortable. A couple of days in the country is great therapy for the stress and exhaustion daily life brings.

It's becoming harder to have contact with the natural world. Buildings are climate controlled, and we seem to treat nature as something to be fought, conquered, or at the very least put up with. If it drips more than three drops of rain, or the temperature is less than balmy, kids are made to stay indoors for recess. Outdoor education classes have all but been eliminated. While it may not be intentional, our children are being cut off from a part of what they are. The connection with the living world gives us completeness, and without it something is missing. Maybe that's why we keep running around looking for material goods, gadgets and comforts to fill the void.

All right, I know you're not likely to be taking your kids off to the mountain to baptize them into nature; but still, a lot can be done. As educators, we sometimes need to take a step back from our scientific outlook. As soon as they enter our school system, we should acquaint our children with the legends and myths of our aboriginal ancestors, with regards to Mother Earth and her treasures. Help them to look at an insect or a plant as a marvel of nature, and not just something to be examined and labelled. Have them grow a garden and tend to it with love. Let them see the glory and power of nature, even at its most damaging, because this is what we come from.

Now the green shift has become part of education, there are more opportunities for schools to grow their own gardens, plant trees and participate in projects which are not only eco-friendly, but which let our kids get their hands in the dirt. Funding is usually available through school boards, eco-friendly groups and even some corporations. There has never been a more ideal time to re-introduce our children to the natural world around them.

Children need to see nature world as an extension of themselves, and they as an element of it. Too often, our science classes tend to present nature as something separate from us, rather than regarding the whole process as a boundless network.

There are many things we can do inside the school. We can invite aboriginals to teach kids to celebrate their harmony with the world through song and dance. They can tell the children stories that can help re-awaken their sense of connection, which although veiled, lives under the mantle of the material world around them.

While most schools teach environmental awareness and promote sustainable actions, this takes us a step deeper. It moves us right into the world outside our man-made walls, where our children can learn to celebrate the rain, the snow, the heat and wind, and see these as marvels of nature, rather than just natural phenomena. We may not be able to spend a week in the countryside, but that doesn't mean our kids can't be baptized into the rich heritage that runs through them. We can help them view the elements as their allies and to respect and live in accord with the world around them. Later, they'll be more likely to appreciate and take joy in the majesty of the natural world and pass it on to their own children.

By helping young people connect with the whole of life, we are bringing them home to regain what they have been missing, so they can feel complete.

CHAPTER THIRTY

The Apple Orchard Syndrome

> Two roads diverged in the woods. I took the one less traveled by, and that has made all the difference.
>
> —Robert Frost, *The Road Not Taken*

The largest slice of my childhood was spent living on the edge of town. At that time the suburbs were not littered with condominiums, box stores and malls. We only needed to walk down the block and cross the road to be in farm country. On those farms were orchards full of juicy sweet apples, pears and peaches, all too tempting for us city boys. After making sure no one was looking, we climbed the fence into the groves of trees.

There, nature unfurled a two-fold treasure. First, stood the best climbing trees around, and second, fresh, ripe, free fruit; the reward for our efforts. Since this was only for sport, we just nicked a couple then headed home. Sometimes we were spotted by the farmer who gave chase, frantically waving his arms and cursing us at the top of his lungs. Naturally, this made the mission all the more thrilling. Once, while taking grapes from a nearby vineyard, we were pursued with a salt gun. Awesome!

I reckon today we would be branded vandals and hauled off for some kind of counselling session. However, I still claim it was a victimless crime, and it made our summers ever so much more exciting than if we had hung about the house all day. That was about as much entertainment as we needed.

At other times, we would pack up a bag with a bottle of pop and a couple of peanut butter sandwiches, (yes, peanut butter), and go on a hike into the forest. This was done with little planning or fanfare. Our parents told us to be careful, not to talk to strangers and such, and be home for supper. Those were golden days, without money, electronics or other outside entertainment. We even had knives and matches. Like the characters in *Stand By Me*, we walked, talked and solved the problems of the world. Then we ate our food and came home. Since there was no such thing as a cell phone, we were out of touch with home for a few hours. I don't think our parents were much bothered about it either.

Today, few kids have an opportunity to experience this kind of simple pleasure. For one thing, the amount of natural space disappears daily. Added to that, parents have too many fears to let them go off by themselves. I suppose if you got through those first two hurdles, you'd have to tackle the final task of finding friends willing to unplug from their gadgets long enough to join.

I call this "The Apple Orchard Syndrome". Kids need their own apple orchard, or at least they need somewhere they can go into nature, to walk, talk and hang with each other. They need a place where video games and television are put to the side, and their only amusement is nature and each other.

Many children come home from school and go directly into their apartment, where they stay until school comes the next day. Much of this is not the fault of parents, as they may live in a built-up area, and for safety reasons want their kids to be home right after school, especially if they're still at work. Meanwhile our children are slowly dying inside, as they become more removed from the world out there, and increasingly hooked into technology. Just in case you missed it the first time; children need an apple orchard!

As educators, we can't do a lot about where kids spend their time out of school hours, but when they are with us we can see to it they have as much time as possible to experience the outdoors. Just take

The Apple Orchard Syndrome

a group of children to a farm where they can jump in the hay and run around the fields, and watch how quickly the instinct for honest, natural fun comes back. That sense has not yet been quenched, but it needs a spark to be rekindled.

Unfortunately, we're in an age where the powers that be, powers that could use a few hours in an apple orchard themselves, consider outdoor education as just another frill. Overnight outdoor trips are more and more endangered due to increasing costs and the fear of lawsuits. Even day trips involve such a myriad of paper work, many find it not worth the hassle. Educators and parents need to remind administration that well rounded, happy kids have to get out of buildings and into nature. This is every bit as, if not more important than covering the academic program. It's in nature that children have a chance to break free from all the layers of technology and information overload.

Anytime spent outside the walls and back in the natural world will benefit the kids, and help rekindle some of that innocent playfulness which is so important during youth. This basic pleasure does wonders for adults as well.

We must insist that our kids have access to the outdoors. Bring parents on board. Let's take some of the money used for technology and academic initiatives, and put it back into meaningful Outdoor Ed. Take your kids out of the class room, and reunite them with the real world. Then they will have their apple orchard, and will be more alive and happy for it.

CHAPTER THIRTY-ONE

Breaking Down the Garden Wall

The wilder the weather is, the more the ravens love it.

—Pema Chodron, *The Wisdom of No Escape*

There is a fable of a man who built a garden high up on a hill, so it could be closer to the sun and the rain. When the flowers began to bloom and the plants gave fruit, he became anxious. He was afraid the hot sun might scorch his plants, and the winds and storms on the mountain could tear them from the ground. In order to protect his patch, he surrounded it with a wall. Seeing that the sun, wind and rain continued to beat down, he built another wall, and yet another. Finally, after he had roofed the whole thing over, he was satisfied everything would be safe.

It wasn't long before he noticed the flowers were beginning to wither and fall from the vines. The stems were starting to discolour and bend. He realized without the sun and the rain, the garden was dying. The only way to save his garden was to remove the roof and knock down the walls. This meant his plants were once again open to the dangers of the elements, but very quickly they revived and flourished.

Life is a dangerous proposition. If you want to live it to its fullest you need to take some risks. Sometimes fears can turn to paranoia

Breaking Down the Garden Wall

and might drive us into ourselves to the point of being unable to face the outside. Too often, we pass these worries on to our children.

We naturally want to protect them and keep them safe from harm. I don't know anyone who would knowingly place kids in dangerous situations. Still, risks are everywhere, and while we're diligent in watching after our children, we cannot, and probably should not try to shelter them from everything. By cocooning them from the world, we become like the gardener. We smother our youth with our fears.

The evidence of excessive worry is all around us. Adventure playgrounds have been stripped down, because they were deemed too dangerous after children started getting hurt. Plus, the skyrocketing number of lawsuits just weren't worth the risk. These have been replaced with scaled-down and equally dull playscapes which minimize the possibility of injury to children. In the process, most of the fun has also been removed. Tetherball poles had the balls removed because children were getting hit in the face. Goggles are required for many team sports in lower grades, and organizing swimming is a nightmare. Sadly, there have been tragedies, but wherever there are children there will be accidents, and while we are vigilant, we must understand that some mishaps are a natural part of growing up. Scrapes, cuts and broken arms will happen, as they have since children learned to walk upright, probably before.

In most schools now, children can't slide down hills or even skate across frozen puddles. Snowballs are outlawed. Students are not allowed to climb trees. Despite this all-out attack on possible mishaps, if you were to go into the office of any school, after any recess, you would still see children lined up to get Band-Aids and ice packs. We may try to eradicate accidents, but we can't guarantee safe play without removing its heart. Children's spirit needs to have excitement. It needs to run and jump and climb and laugh. If we try to bundle kids up and shield them from all danger, we also suffocate that spirit. We instill our anxiety in them and teach them to be as neurotic as we are.

When we consider safety, it's important to maintain the balance between care and smothering. This requires the move from unreasonable fear, to healthy protection of children.

TEACHING IN THE SPIRIT

The moment our children are out of our sight, there's a degree of risk. While no one is suggesting our youngsters should be unattended, there comes a time when we have to let go to some degree. We have to open a hole in a few of the walls so our children have a chance to breathe, and feel the sun, the wind and the rain. If you think about it, our kid's sedentary life-style poses a much bigger health hazard than climbing an apple tree.

It isn't an easy jump. It's hard to let go. We all love our children and don't want them to come to any harm, but for the sake of keeping the heart and wonder of childhood alive, we must take a small leap of faith and break down some of the garden walls.

CHAPTER THIRTY-TWO

Lightening Up

> But what is harmony except the simple harmony between a man and the life he leads.
>
> —Albert Camus, *The Stranger*

It took about a year of teaching to become confident and cocky enough to survive middle school students. While I cannot overemphasize the value of honest respect, I've never believed in political correctness for its own sake. Helping my kids see a sense of the ridiculous was always a kind of mission and it sometimes meant crossing the line of what many consider appropriate. For this, I make no apologies. My first grade 8 class understood that my humour was all in good fun and especially enjoyed it when the spotlight shone on them.

Our Science class was a small Noah's Ark of wildlife. The kids loved the animals and waited in line to take them home for the holidays. Oddly enough, it seems allergies weren't such a huge issue in those days.

I had one class that was quite sharp and had a good sense of humour. This means they got my jokes. It was a fairly multi-cultural group, and I had fun gently teasing them about their nationalities without anyone getting upset, at least to my knowledge. I included my own English birth in the mix. One boy had the splendid Dutch name, Vandervoort. I kidded him about liking chocolate and such. At Christmas when I was farming out the animals, J. asked if he could take the pet lizard home for the holidays. I told him it was no problem as long as he had a note from his mum. The next day he arrived in class looking very pleased with himself and handed me this message:

"Dear Mr. Porter;

Of course, J. may bring home the lizard for the holidays and don't you worry about anything. If he gets cold he can climb into my wooden shoes, and if he gets thirsty I can give him plenty of hot chocolate.

Sincerely,
Mrs. V

I read the letter, burst into a laugh and told J. that his mother was the best. He was tickled over the whole thing. And guess what? Nobody was upset! Years later when I was asked to speak at a retirement function, there was applause when I offered, "Being offended is a choice, not an obligation." It was comforting to see others were also weary of the modern-day phobia of affronting people, or folks who make an occupation out of being victims.

Somewhere along the way life became a very serious, sombre affair. People work long hours, and are satisfied to keep to themselves and families after work. It's not often you people celebrating out in the streets, as they do in many other cultures. Festivity is generally reserved for Christmas or other such holidays. Vacation time is minimal compared to many other nations of this world. More and more, corporations make increased demands on their employees, to the point where they are electronically chained to the office, even when they aren't there physically. Lunch is often eaten at office desks in order to keep up with the work load. I felt badly for the parents of my kids who would be docked a day's pay if they needed to stay home because their child was sick.

If you take a look at the average neighbourhood in Western Society, you see very little to indicate that people are rejoicing in the

Lightening Up

dance of life. This, despite the fact we have so much more than most of the world. The suburban streets empty at night, as families hide behind their walls, often catching up on office work or plugged in to their toys.

Except for occasional festivals, few streets vibrate with the tastes, smells and sounds of revelry. Life has become a sober affair, and one of the first things we do is hand down the notion that getting by is tough, and you need to work hard to keep up.

We often tend to scoff at societies which run on a more relaxed time frame, places where productivity and profit are not seen as the main measure of success. In the modern world, siestas, long lunches and vacations decrease efficiency, and that's bad for business.

This contagion of busyness has spread into our classrooms, where harried teachers try desperately to keep up with the expectations; objectives made by people who have been away from childhood and its wonders for so long they've forgotten the magic of youth. Anything non-academic, even birthday parties is considered a waste of valuable learning time. The list of goals is endless and teachers are constantly in panic mode, for fear of not completing the curriculum. Humour is conspicuously absent in case someone feels insulted, and it shows in our kids. We equate hard work with success. On the surface that may seem fine, but our definition of success lacks one huge component; joy.

We load kids down with assignments and homework. Students spend increasingly long hours in front of faceless, emotionless computers. We convince them the more facts they gather, the more power they'll have. Yes, we might be preparing our kids for life, but the life we are preparing them for is likely to be just as unfulfilling as those of the adults who shuffle through their days, half asleep.

Many times, I have been in classrooms where frustrated teachers are becoming agitated because their kids are merely acting as kids. Wonderful opportunities to laugh and enjoy moments together are missed, when we forget to lighten up and see the simple joy of each moment, the pleasures of being alive.

When we're completely caught up in our own small world, we fail to truly see the things that are real. Everything we experience is coloured by our own disappointments, fears and wishes. As teachers, if we step back from all the chaos we perceive going on in our lives, and consider the enormity of life, we will open ourselves to the wonderful gifts our profession has to offer.

Our entire way of perceiving reality has to shift. Be it through meditation, yoga or other means of slowing ourselves down, we can start to lighten up. We can see that much of what we think is so important, means very little in the larger picture. When we can do this, we begin to appreciate each moment we spend with our children. Once we see things this way, our entire way of teaching relaxes. There are goals to meet, but the world will not end if we don't achieve them all. We can be creative and have fun along the way.

Society needs to make this fundamental change in perception. If more of us in education start to slow down and cheer up in our lives, our view of learning will start to change. We will realize classrooms can be places of fun, laughter and joy; places in which children take delight, where adult and child share a common secret; that life is a dance and we are all partners.

Too often, our schools are rated by the results of standardized tests, the number of kids on the honour role, or their percentage of graduates and where they go when they enter the working world. Some witless politicians have the ridiculous idea of instituting merit pay for teachers. Beyond the numbers, how do you measure an exemplary instructor? How many schools are measured by the happiness of the students? Can we really quantify the amount of creativity the staff put into their lessons, and the depth of imagination of the children?

There is no scale to evaluate the feeling of peaceful, loving energy that pervades certain classes and schools. Since these things are not tangible, they often are dismissed when we evaluate education.

The simple truth is we need to remember how to have fun, how to laugh, and bring real meaning into the classroom. No test scores or academic achievement can ever have more importance than this.

CHAPTER THIRTY-THREE

What Is Really Best for Them?

> My boy's gonna play in the big league.
>
> —Tom Cochrane

When I was young, I had a few friends who had a lot of trouble with school. They'd been kept back a couple of times, as was the custom then, but their parents were convinced that with a bit of extra work, they'd turn things around, go to post-secondary and be successful. The fact is, school just wasn't their cup of tea. So they left the class room and took an early turn in the work world. Some started out as apprentices and others found work where they could. Without going into the details, eventually nearly all of them found their niche, acquired some needed skills, and landed in good positions without the benefit of higher education. This came from finding their own paths, not those of the well-intentioned, but somewhat misguided adults in their life.

There are countless stories of parents who sacrifice everything for the sake of laying a good foundation for their kids. Sometimes it may be the teachers who try to steer their students towards a destination they believe is the right one. But there's a caveat here. What you think is best for your children, may not be the path for which they are most suited.

While we want our kids to have a happy, fulfilling life and career, there's a risk we're pushing our own projections and goals onto them. While you're busy making plans for your kid's life, you need to take a long, hard look and ask yourself who you're trying to make happy. Maybe the old clichés about work, marriage and retirement don't work for everyone. Our path may not be theirs. We've all seen the fanatical hockey parent who is convinced their child is going to make it to the big leagues. A lot of that attitude can stem from that parent's own insecurity, maybe a need for validation.

Exposing students to various career choices is fine, and may spark a flame. But must we rush them into selecting their future long before they are ready? Many people reach adulthood without a chosen field, only to discover their path seemingly by chance. If a young person is sure of the direction they want to go, then by all means nurture their dream, but let's not make our aspirations theirs.

Whose dream is it for Johnny to become a lawyer or a doctor? Why is it so important to us? Is it not more meaningful that each child experiences the most opportunities for growth, right now? When we approach each day in this manner, the future takes care of itself.

As teachers, part of our mandate is to help guide young people into the adult world with a sense of direction and the aptitudes and tools needed to achieve their goals. We can give them the confidence to make decisions about their own future. If they're not ready for that, we need to step aside and concede it may not be the right time, yet.

While we can't foresee where our kids will be when they are adults, we can be observant enough to notice where students gravitate in their interests and abilities. When we see a child is particularly talented, or totally engaged in a certain activity, we need to nourish this attraction without forcing the issue. Avoid making expectations that are not reasonable, and help parents understand what they imagine to be best for their child's future, may not be the one that suits them. Ultimately, each child will discover where they will go in this life. As teachers and parents, we have to find that balance between helping our kids reach their fullest potential, and supporting them in their decisions, even if they are not the ones we would choose.

What Is Really Best for Them?

The hardest part is having the courage and faith to let them stumble and fall sometimes, because it's there perhaps, they will make their greatest discoveries.

CHAPTER THIRTY-FOUR

Letting Go of The Reins

> You may give them your love, but not your thoughts. For they have their own thoughts. You may house their bodies, but not their souls. For their souls dwell in the house of tomorrow, which you cannot visit, even in your dreams. You may strive to be like them, but seek not to make them like you.
>
> —Kahlil Gibran, *The Prophet*

When I was in elementary school, the most terrifying thing that could happen to you was to be sent to the principal's office. This was truly the end of the line. In a scene reminiscent of the first encounter between Dorothy and the Wizard of Oz, you would practice your grovel as you approached, with visions of the unspeakable horrors awaiting you. Nothing good ever came from a visit to the principal.

Today, a visit to the principal may still involve a stern lecture, but it also might be to receive praise for a job well done. The big boss might give you a special assignment for which you have a unique talent, such as recording a school event. Our whole outlook of going to the principal's office has shifted with the way we look at discipline, and there have been many changes indeed. Our modus operandi has shifted from the stifling suppressive regimen of Victorian times, to the laissez-faire philosophy of the 70's, plus a number of models in between and since. No amount of debate can ever assess the most effective method, because there is no quantitative measurement. We have however, learned those models which are ineffective and counter-productive, and for the most part abandoned them.

I suppose we might count up the number of school infractions, or look at the orderliness of classrooms. We could see who has the straightest, quietest lines in the halls, and compare test results; but in the end, we know these are not gauges of effective classroom management. Prison has a pretty strict regulation system, but that doesn't ensure when someone is released they will act skilfully in the world, any better than someone brought up with a completely Bohemian lifestyle.

The fact is, we can make and implement some very harsh rules and see immediate changes in conduct, but they are superficial and unlikely to endure once the controls are relaxed. That's because our desire to do the right thing, to live more impeccably, doesn't come from outside forces. It comes from our sense of belonging and feeling accountable for more than just ourselves.

When we feel our bond with the rest of the world, it shifts us into a position of awesome responsibility to the whole. Then we start to lose our sense of self-importance, our need to gain at other's expense. We see that when we hurt others, we damage everyone, including ourselves. Once we are aware of the power of our every action and thought, we're less likely to act in a way which may harm others.

It's natural to be kinder and gentler towards others when we feel comfortable in our skin, more at peace, in touch with and aware of our actions and feelings. This doesn't always come easily. By the time we meet our students, they've already had years to develop their own mind-set, which may not be particularly altruistic.

So we won't start throwing all the rule books out the window and expecting kids to automatically act in an exemplary fashion. One thing is certain; if we guide our children to be self-aware, where they don't feel they're in a struggle with life; self-regulation will come as naturally as breathing. This won't be because someone has laid down a book full of rules, but because a sense of living and moving with clarity has become integrated into their whole being. Acting in a more loving, caring and harmonious manner will be part of how they live, because it's already part of what they are. Then like the hundredth monkey, it will become part of the field, and there will be less need for a mountain of rules.

This is the beautiful side benefit of nurturing and teaching the whole child. Authority and management become less necessary, because as our children feel their life is a comfortable fit, they live more mindfully, learning to act with greater compassion.

Most of the Native North American Nations had little time for written laws and penal codes. They knew their connection and duty to the Earth and each other. Living life harmoniously was second nature. Transgressions of course, occurred, but were not the norm. Today, it seems society works on the assumption people that don't know how to act, and they need rules to guide them through life's basic actions. To prove the point, take a look at the procedures for even the simplest of organizations. Check out your bank card contract. What about the embarrassing disclaimers on television commercials?

Until we shift the way we look at life, our world will be full of edicts. On the other hand, as we become more perceptive and pass it on to our children, law and order will come more from each individual, until it become a seamless way to live. It appears to be a long stretch, but many civilizations in corners of the world where greed, materialism and video voyeurism don't dictate lifestyle; have lived that way for generations, and continue to do so.

Take stock of some of the minor demands you insist on. Are they really serving any purpose, or are they merely old habits you've been holding onto? Have they been passed on by your mentors or are they a hangover from your own school days? As you teach your kids to be more in touch with their actions, with a more expansive view of their world, you may be able to let go of some of the rules. Having done that, you might also find your kids are capable of self-management to a degree you never thought possible. If it's too early, you can simply say, "Hey guys, I thought we could do this, but maybe we aren't ready, so let's keep working on it."

Kids continue to need boundaries and limits, but we have to step back and see when direction is necessary and when we can relax. We need to decide which guidance comes from honesty and what is merely self-serving and egocentric. The greatest teaching we can give, lies in guiding our children towards internal regulation. When that happens, we will fully share with kids the experience of discovery and learning, because we won't be caught up in unnecessary control issues and petty power struggles.

CHAPTER THIRTY-FIVE

The Wonder Years

> Education has no meaning unless it helps us to understand the vast expanse of life, with all its subtleties, with all its multi-faceted beauty, its sorrows and joys.
>
> —Jane Bay, *Precious Jewels of Tibet*

Before the modern age of science, people looked up at the skies and pondered the strange lights, flashes of lightning and the cracks of thunder. Sunrise and sunset were a time for rituals of thanksgiving and awe. Adventurous souls gazed longingly across the wide oceans and wondered what lay beyond. Life was a great mystery. Still today for a young child, every new flower or flake of snow is an event.

The human mind is inherently curious. The secrets of our Earth and beyond have been explored over the centuries, until there's little in the physical world that hasn't been studied inside out. But this has a down side. While solving the mysteries of the universe has opened door ways for human kind, it has also shut the gateway which opens the world to the miraculous. The exploration and study of nature may enhance our knowledge, but the trade-off is we lose some of the numinous.

The Wonder Years

When everything is rationalized with logic and fact, a hole is created. Our ability to be amazed and astonished at the world is stunted. Life becomes clinical and scientific. Then we start to miss what I call, the simple fantastic. How many people stop to savour the smell of the rain or watch the ever-changing majesty of the clouds? Who takes a moment to observe insects as they go about their daily activities? We may see the heavens at night, but do we truly grasp the amazing expanse and mystery of our universe?

It's sad to see, but there are not many children who will look away from their televisions or video games and become excited at a rainbow or a sunset. Nor will adults for that matter. Kids are encouraged to look at DVDs while they are being whisked past magnificent scenery in their SUV's, rather than appreciating the wonders of this Earth. The problem is, once the excitement of life has been quenched, it isn't easily re-kindled.

Just because the world has been largely explored and nature has been analyzed, this doesn't depreciate its wonder and value. I know the causes of a rainbow. The big bang fascinates me. I appreciate the scientific significance of Higgs boson. But, do you know what? The explanation of these phenomena pales when compared to the mere wonders of creation. No video games, pay for view shows, mansions or sports cars can match the magnificence of a flock of geese coming in for a landing over water. No music man can produce, can match the sound of rain on a roof, or the silence of snow falling in the forest.

It's our duty as teachers to see our children don't become so lost in modern technology and the pursuit of information that they stop experiencing this sense of amazement over life. If they do, they are doomed to miss some of the most awesome moments existence has to offer. We don't have to stand by and let this happen.

Whenever you can, get the kids outside to experience the world. You don't even have to leave the school area. Turn off the air conditioning, open the windows and listen to the rain, feel the freshness of the wind. Smell the flowers in the spring. Watch snowflakes as they fall. Remind your kids that although science can explain how the parts of a flower function, no one can completely understand the inscrutable workings of nature. When teaching Healthy Living, have the kids think deeply about how the body works, beyond the mechanical. The miracle of eyesight, hearing. No matter how much knowledge we have, there will always be an element of the unknowable.

The discovery and knowledge of science are a testament to humankind's resourcefulness, but their study should in no way negate the wonders and mysteries of life. No matter how much we explore, questions will remain unanswered.

Teachers aren't fond of saying they don't know so they may avoid or trivialize such mysteries as crop circles, King Arthur, or UFO's. Don't be afraid to jump into these kinds of enigmas. Let the kids say what they think, and then, and this is the hardest part for many of us, be willing to let the discussion end at that. Admit that scientists really don't know everything, nor do you, and that's part of the fun. Someone once said, "I believe in unicorns." And what harm is there in that?

Much of nature has been explained and reasoned until everything wonderful and magic is gone. We have the opportunity to rekindle the sense of newness a child experiences when he first explores his world. It's a world where everything is fresh and exciting and remains so until the balloon is deflated with logic and facts. Give kids the facts, but remind them that no matter how much we research and learn, or how much we read, life remains a mystery, and that is something to keep you excited and grateful for each day.

But remember, if you are hoping to pass this on to your kids, you are probably due for a refresher course in The Wonder of Life 101. If you don't feel it yourself, they'll also have trouble buying into it. Get out there and reacquaint yourself with all that is simply fantastic and then pass it on.

CHAPTER THIRTY-SIX

Silence

> Stop speaking and let spirit
> speak through you.
>
> —Rumi

Before the pencil pushers in high places decided outdoor education was a frill, the highlight of the school year was the three-day trip to the field centre. Our first evening hike began as a boisterous mix of excited voices, squeals, and innocent laughter. Nervous chatter masked fears of being in the dark. At one point, the field center instructor asked the children to stand still and be totally quiet for a moment. Not an easy task for the average eleven-year-old. When a hush finally settled over the kids, they were amazed to find themselves in a whole new world. Asked what they heard, they excitedly pointed out the rustle of the leaves, the creak of trees in the wind, the crack of old branches, hoot of an owl, even their own breathing! For many of them this was a first, brief glimpse into the beauty of silence.

Silence is not a popular commodity in today's' society. The modern world is filled with noise, from the sounds of traffic and the hum of machinery, to the constant prattle of voices. There are few places left where you can get away from all this racket. Not only do we manufacture all of this incessant din, but we pretty much discourage quiet. Our gadgets and toys guarantee any peace will be chased away. Radios are constantly blaring. Video games, computers and televisions shatter what could be the sanctuary of our homes. People walk in nature with ears and eyes glued to their phones, totally oblivious to the display of beauty around them. The peaceful, potentially healing sounds of nature are blotted out. Birdsong, the rustle of the breeze and the laughing sounds of a rushing stream get submerged in the assault of technology. It seems we'll do anything to avoid being alone with ourselves.

This is the culture we are passing to our children. Most kids never experience true stillness, and so they become comfortable with noise. It's easier to keep a child pacified with a game or TV, than trying to engage them in more creative pursuits such as reading, drawing or building. In this we do children a huge disservice. We deny them the healing and rejuvenating power of silence and lead them to believe they must be plugged in at all times. This isn't our natural state. Watch how quietly a very young child plays when he's on his own. It's inborn.

Remember, the more children are connected to the world of technology, the more they buy into society's myths. Then they're less likely to become free, reflective thinkers.

Fortunately, there's a lot we can do to fix this. We can help children enrich themselves through silence. In my classes we would often take a moment to sit silently and experience our senses. Suddenly the kids could hear their breathing, detect subtle changes in the lighting, or hear the air conditioning. For a few moments they were waking up. Think how much our kids could benefit from going outside and spending some time experiencing the sounds of nature. What if there was a quiet ten minutes every day, where children reflected and perhaps later, talked about, wrote, or even drew what they felt?

Of course, there are times when we discourage sounds to help children concentrate. Don't think of this as being true silence. When the mind is engaged in academic activity, there can be no chance of achieving real quiet. Silence means letting go of the thinking process for a while. On the other hand, there's no need to eliminate distractions. If there is noise from traffic or chatter from another room, so be it. That's part of the occasion. All the children need to do is calm themselves, maybe take a few breaths, or close their eyes and observe what happens. Parents would also find the home to be a more peaceful place if they planned a similar activity, if only for a few minutes.

By using these steps, our kids may stop avoiding silence and start appreciating, even welcoming it. It's a small move on the road to finding out a little more about themselves. Without all of this commotion, they have a true chance to be more creative and aware of the world around them. Their minds become a little more spacious. That opens the door to a whole world of discovery.

CHAPTER THIRTY-SEVEN

Remembering the Sacred

> Beauty is the religion of the sages.
>
> —Kahlil Gibran

Some mornings I arrived at work, and realized my drive was a blank. I'd barely noticed the weather, the smell of the air as I walked to my car, or the music I listened to along the way. Never mind the traffic. It's a wonder I arrived in one piece. The trip to work had become a throw away, just a means to an end, a forty-minute slice of my life in the discard pile.

I still lapse, but now before I get into the car, I breathe in the air, look at the sky, feel the wind. I drive mindfully and enjoy the ride. Now each trip is a little fresher.

Much of our time is spent waiting for something else, a stepping stone to something we consider more enjoyable or important. We dash through our morning ablutions in order to be on the road before peak traffic. For much of the workday, we grudgingly perform our duties, waiting until we can return home, relax, and enjoy some quality time. Even that downtime might be peppered with distractions, such as television, computers, phone calls and home work.

Remembering the Sacred

How much of our lives is spent with our mind engaged with other things, like getting ready to go somewhere, commuting, wolfing down a quick lunch or waiting in queues? We dash through our daily activities as if they were a giant shopping list to be crossed off until it's finished. All the while, we're only partly present, at best.

If this isn't bad enough, we're not content to live in our own neuroses. We infect our kids. From the moment they're able to do anything by themselves, we tell children to hurry up, not waste time. But is that what they're really doing? Is it possible a child is simply savouring a moment, absorbed in what they are doing? Rushing is not a habit they're born with. It needs to be taught. Kids are coached into believing particular activities are more important than others. We cajole them into completing certain tasks with the promise of something better later on.

"Finish your supper and then you can play." Right away, we imply eating is trivial, and playing is the payoff.

The advertising industry cashes in on this idiosyncrasy. Your gadgets and aps will help you multi-task, accomplishing even greater amounts of work. But what is multi-tasking, other than doing several things superficially? How sad it is that parents need to placate their kids with movies or tablets on a road trip, so they won't be bored. It makes the trip a means to an end, something to get over with the least pain possible. When I was a child, the trip to the cottage was half the fun. We played games like *I Spy*, counted cows and cars. We punched, squabbled and had a ball. Despite the cliché, we didn't whine, "Are we there yet?"

Getting ready for school or bed is not just a bunch of chores to complete, in order to move on to the next order of business. Eating isn't something to be done with the clock ticking and a lunchroom supervisor telling kids to hurry up, so everyone can go outside. Daily school routines have their high or active points and lower-paced, less lively times, but everything has its place and is worth taking the time to enjoy.

All we do can be done with mindfulness. The sacred is all around if we slow down. The mad pace of the world is not something our kids should be inheriting until they're as time obsessed as the rest of us. When they're little, children know how to live in the moment. Watch a baby observing her world. She's in no hurry.

Yes, the world does work on clock time, and there are deadlines to be met and appointments to keep. But this doesn't mean the journey to get there is any less important. As we remind ourselves to be more in the moment and give our attention to all we do, we can help our children maintain that gift of mindfulness. Maybe we only have an hour for lunch, but we needn't blast through it without any consciousness. We can still slow down, eat mindfully and feel the benefit. Nutritionists have long touted the value of mindful eating in maintaining a healthy diet. Our brain may see the deadline, without turning it into an obsession. Like it or not, our time on this earth has a limit, so the last thing we should be doing is discounting any part of life.

Parents can start by making bedtime special. Don't turn it into a battle. Even if you're worn out, these moments can be filled with fun and tenderness, where we can kick back and savour the day that has passed, enjoy the subtle sounds, smells and sights of nighttime. Morning can be a time to look forward to a new day, be grateful we're alive, and let the senses feel. If you're thinking this is easy for me to say, believe me, I've been there, making everything into a task or battle. I guarantee the alternative is the better way.

Teachers can ask their kids to be observant on the way to school and report what they experienced to the class. We might occasionally stop during the day to be quiet and feel the world around us. Like monks, we might ring a bell once in a while to help us all come back to the present moment.

And while this is happening, the world will continue to turn. We can still be on time, make our appointments, but we'll relax and live each moment along the way. Nothing is mundane. Adults need to rediscover the miracle of being alive. This is a piece of our social DNA that needn't be passed on to the next generation. If we are totally awake in our own lives, we will help our children live in the present, enjoying each moment as it comes and goes.

CHAPTER THIRTY-EIGHT

Before You Take Another Step

> If you can get out of your own way, you won't be in anyone else's.
>
> —Aldous Huxley, *The Island*

Have you ever had a friend give you a concerned look and ask, "Are you all right?" or "Is something the matter?" Yes, you feel fine. Why are they asking? On the flip side, has there been a time when you felt someone's anguish stabbing straight through you, even though they hadn't spoken a word?

The simple ups and downs of life place us under pressure much of the time. At times we feel it through to our core. Sometimes it simmers, hidden below the surface, just waiting for a chance to come to the boil, and then some small upset comes along and we're yelling at the dog. Although we may feel at total balance and riding along with the world, inside, the strain of everyday life can be piling up and wearing us down. At these times, those who are a bit more vulnerable may catch our feelings before we do.

Our tensions, stress and anger toward the world are an almost palpable energy, one which we can pass on like a virulent virus, affecting everyone with whom we come into contact. People do feel our mood, emotions, and passions. Some are so susceptible they feel the energy of someone entering a room, two doors away.

Imagine now how this can affect our colleagues and the young children in our care. This makes it essential that those of us who deal with children every day, find some balance in our lives, whether it be through meditation, exercise, yoga, hobbies, or simple self-reflection. The bottom line being, we don't want to be creating disharmony or chaos from the energy we're projecting.

Many cultures throughout history have understood the importance of this, and that is why before entering someone's house it was traditional to pause for a moment and say a prayer or make an offering. This was a chance to clear away some of the lower or coarse vibrations before taking them into another's living space. Removing the shoes is another token of respect, and a way of leaving the energy of the world out there; out there.

Most of us just barge into people's houses or our work space, without realizing the mess of feelings we are bringing with us. Think of the anxiety that's wrought from a simple commute to work. What are we bringing from home? How much discord results from watching the news or crime shows? This is our baggage and we're about to dump it in front of the first person we meet.

Before you enter someone's space, in a teacher's case this is the classroom; take the time to clear yourself. This can be as simple as sitting quietly in the parking lot for a moment. Maybe, say a couple of words, take a breath or two. Five minutes listening to a favourite song might do the trick. Whatever fits will do. When you clear do so in complete selflessness. Recognize when you may not be sending out the best dynamics and do whatever it takes to avoid infecting others with your negativity. Your only motivation is for others to receive the best from you and for you to not affect them in an obstructive way.

This goes for meetings with colleagues as well. Remember, what you pass on to your fellow workers, reaches the kids. It's all about respecting the space and feelings of others. I assume your main purpose for working with young people is to make a positive difference in their lives. The last thing you want to do is unwittingly set up hurdles.

Before You Take Another Step

The best thing about learning something new is passing it on. Try some simple clearing exercises with your kids. When things get too hectic or tense, stop for a moment and breathe together. Have them make a calming affirmation or sing a song. After lunch take five minutes to let the kids put their heads down and unwind. Share some relaxing music. Be creative. There are many ways to create a peaceful tone, and from experience, I know the kids love it. Blasting ahead into activity when no one is ready, serves no one.

We need to find balance in our lives, both for ourselves and for our students. However, unless we are masters, we're going to be affected by the world in which we live. The simple act of emptying ourselves can help release some of that chaos, before we pass it on to those we most care most about.

CHAPTER THIRTY-NINE

What Do Your Children See?

> Setting an example is not the main means of influencing another, it is the only way.
>
> —Albert Einstein

In an old country and western classic, a child, tired of the fighting and arguing going on between his parents, says to his friend, "I don't want to play house." Okay, this is just a country tear jerker. Or is it also a reflection of how bad adult conduct can affect our kids? Ask yourself, how much adult behavior would you want your kids want to emulate?

While many teachers won't admit it, they still embody the old cliché. "Do as I say, not as I do." I'm sure most teachers truly believe they are trying to model exemplary behaviour in all of their actions. This is where the problems start. Since many us have never taken the time to self-reflect, we go on throwing our idiosyncrasies, moods and biases at our kids. While we may not do these things willfully, our students are stuck with us for six hours each day, and children are very receptive.

Of course, no one is suggesting you change your entire personality, or try to attain perfection. You are who you are. But the act of being aware of the scope of your influence on kids is potentially

What Do Your Children See?

transforming. It's not just the things you say, or even your actions in the classroom which affect your students. Your entire outlook on life, the way you handle yourself throughout the day. This energy radiates from you. These are the things your children pick up on, whether they are conscious of it or not.

Life isn't an easy gig. There are pressures, hardships, disappointments, and general annoyances, which are all part of the journey. If you work as a linesman for the phone company out in the countryside, you may not have to worry about the effect you have on others at work. On the other hand, when you spend your day dealing closely with others, and you're hoping to make a positive difference, you'd better be sure that what you are bringing to the table is palatable.

That's why it's so important that those of us involved in young people's lives take the time to do some soul searching. This kind of reflection helps us to see some of our motivations. Living our day from a standpoint of awareness, we're able to observe how we conduct ourselves, and how we act and react as we go through each moment, every occurrence. This doesn't mean sitting in judgment, condemning our behaviour, or for that matter indulging in narcissism. It simply means we pay attention to what we do, and see what we're bringing from our personal lives into the classroom. We move beyond all our posturing. Then, instead of trying to set what we think is a good example, we act with honesty. At this point, we can trust our actions and know it's enough.

Maybe, you'll find out the calm you thought you displayed all the time was in fact a sham, and the kids have picked up an entirely different message. Perhaps, they were feeling the anger you thought was hidden. How were you feeling inside when you talked about caring and compassion? Witnessing feelings as they arise is the perfect opportunity to discover more about ourselves. I caution you, you won't always like what you find, but that's not what counts. What's important is that now, instead of just blundering through the day, you start to see what's going on beneath the surface. Having done this, you will know how to proceed.

Another place to start is by looking at the way we are running our lives outside of the classroom. Are we giving ourselves quiet time for contemplation? Are we keeping in touch with nature, taking a few moments each day for meditation or true relaxation? Do we allow ourselves to come to a more centered place, so what we bring into the lives of other children is supportive?

Most enter the teaching profession in order to have a constructive effect in young lives. However, if emotionally and spiritually we are in turmoil, or if we are so full of ourselves that there is no room in our hearts for our kids, our influence is not going to be what we hoped for. No matter how professional we are; no matter how much training and experience we have, and no matter how honourable our intentions; we won't live up to that lofty goal.

If you're hoping to teach compassion, peace, respect, self-worth, and dignity, you must be coming from a place where all of those qualities live. A good starting point is taking time to take a frank look at yourself. Then you can determine where you are right now and where it is you need to go. That doesn't mean you need to enroll in the first yoga class you can find, although it may be a fit for you personally. It, rather, involves reflecting on the way you operate your life, and openly evaluating what you are offering to the students. Once you are sure it is honest and filled with compassion, you are ready to lift that to a higher place.

CHAPTER FORTY

How Do You See the Child?

> Perhaps teaching is really mutual experience between the younger and the older. Perhaps all that is to be learned is what they can discover between them.
>
> —Amanda Cross, *The Theban Mysteries*

I'd like you to ponder a couple of simple questions. The only proviso is that you are completely honest. Ask yourself, "What kind of relationship do I want to have with my students?" Having answered that, try this, "How do I really feel about kids?" These are pretty open-ended questions, but your first reactions can reveal a lot about yourself and whether teaching is really your calling.

The truth is, there are many adults who hold a superior and patronizing attitude towards youth. Recall the movies you've watched, or books have you read, where the adults have a problem which they cannot solve. Lo and behold, along comes a young child trying to give his suggestions, only to be shushed because he's only a kid. In the end of course, to the amazement of all the big people, he's the one who comes up with the solution.

Throughout history, children have been abused, used as cheap labour, and treated as belongings. Sometimes they have been merely tolerated, expected to be seen and not heard. Of course, on the other side of the coin, we know children are also cherished and treated with great tenderness and love. Yet our youth are often viewed as if they are in a different league from the rest of the population. Seniors seem to suffer the same complaint. It's as if children have to incubate pending adulthood, where they become useful citizens, and remain so until they become seniors and are marginalized once again.

Rites of passage throughout the ages have heralded the onset of adulthood as if the caterpillar had suddenly become a butterfly. While many of these rites have cultural and spiritual value, they also reinforce duality and separation. Many teachers treat childhood as a disease they can cure. The attitude being, "With my personal guidance and experience, I will help these children become good adults. Like me." As long as there's this illusion of separation between the grown-up and the student, it's hard for school to be an illuminating experience. Two-way learning can't operate in this paradigm.

One way to remove this barrier and other dualities, is to remember we all come from the same source. People may act badly, but they are neither good nor bad. We may win and lose at certain endeavours, but there are no winners or losers. Ultimately children and adults are the same, and kids do not need the adults to fix them. We're all traveling on a journey. As grown-ups, we have more life practice, and so have a duty to pass it on. This doesn't make us superior or separate, nor does it make everything we know right. It merely makes us a co-author in this story, with our particular role as guide.

Always be awake, aware of the way you are thinking and acting towards the children. If your outlook is not one of equanimity, then some changes need to happen. This isn't easy, especially when there have been years of developing some hard-set notions and opinions. Through deep seeing, we can learn to discard our worn-out ideas and see all living beings as equal, with no one above or below. When this happens, we approach our students with an unbiased view and we're capable of guiding them more effectively, because we aren't looking though a clouded lens. When we see children as fellow partners in the human experience, the message we deliver becomes infinitely more meaningful and accessible.

CHAPTER FORTY-ONE

Can You Hear Me?

> When you meet your friend on the roadside, let the voice within your voice speak to the ear of his ear.
>
> —Kahlil Gibran, *The Prophet*

One of my classrooms was the last outpost on the way to the playground. It was well stocked with games, toys and sports equipment. Many of the kids dropped by on their way out the door. Sometimes it was just to say hello, and at other times, to borrow something.

One fine spring morning, Johnny and Freddy, regular grade two customers, arrived at the start of lunch recess. Johnny, a charmer with the most enchanting, yet devilish smile ever possessed by a child, burst into the room and in the process of grabbing a ball, said, "Can I have a ball?"

Always trying to instil at least a few crumbs of civility into the kids, I said, "Pardon?" waiting for the magic word which always opened the door to the riches of our stash.

Having heard my question, Johnny responded, "Can I have a ball?"

Changing my approach, I said, "I can't hear you."

Obliging me, he once again asked, "Can I have a ball?"

Seeing that this approach was leading us nowhere, I focused my attention on Freddy. I looked him squarely in the eye and said, "What does Johnny need to say to get a ball?"

Without missing a beat, he looked up at me, cupped his hands and screamed in his loudest voice, "Can he have a ball?"

Sometimes kids just want to be heard. The fact is, everyone wants to know that someone, somewhere is listening. Here, lies the root of communication breakdowns. Most people hear what's being said to them, but not as many are really listening.

If we're to truly connect with our children, and let them know they are valued and important, we need to practice deep listening.

Many teachers will insist they are indeed good listeners, and on a surface level that may hold some merit. However, we have to ask ourselves if we are really hearing our kids, or if rather we are so wrapped up in circumstances, judgments and handing out appropriate consequences, we overlook what they're trying to tell us.

Our mind is frequently so engaged in planning what's about to come out of our mouths, we miss what others are trying to say. True listening is not as common as you might think. The words being spoken are not the whole message. Mastering our mind's ramblings is not the easiest thing to do, so the kind of listening we usually manage is superficial at best. We often don't catch meaning conveyed in other ways. This generates misunderstandings between people, and is the cause of all manner of conflicts.

When we deep listen, we don't engage in a private conversation in our heads, neither do we judge, or try to figure what clever advice we can give. We are merely listening. When we start to listen without comment or mental commentary, something wonderful happens; we catch what the other person is saying on many levels. We hear beyond the immediate circumstances and start to see motives and feelings beyond the words. Listening with a compassionate ear gives us a better picture about what's going on with that other person.

Once we've actually listened, without intrusions from our old habits and presumptions, we can act much more effectively and skilfully. We avoid making rash judgments and decisions we may soon come to regret. Our kids then begin to trust us enough to open up and let us in on what is happening in their lives. With trust will come a greater degree of truthfulness. A child who feels comfortable enough to be honest, will feel happier and more at ease.

Deep listening does not come easily, as we've probably built up a circuit of old habits, which need to be rewired. By being totally aware when we engage with someone, we recognize when we're judging, or our attention has wandered. In that moment of focus, we automatically and gently return to our listening. As we listen deeply, we naturally tune in to the unspoken feelings and words from the other half of our conversation. Now we aren't just conversing, we are meeting.

Before you start to engage with a child, see them as a fellow being, neither above or below you. Recognize their basic innocence, and appreciate there are reasons behind their actions and moods. There may be pain you've not noticed in your haste during past dealings. When you look at the child this way, you view the exchange from a position of complete openness. Then you're less likely to judge or be critical, and likely to act with compassion and insight. This is how you build relationships which have meaning.

CHAPTER FORTY-TWO

Pass the Bottle

> The seeds of anger are always there, but when you notice, when you keep alive your understanding, they have no chance to manifest.
>
> —Thich Nhat Hahn, *Interbeing*

The bell signals the end of recess. Moments later, three kids burst into the room screaming at each other. Accusations fly, language borders on blue and there is a definite danger of it getting physical. Even Doctor Phil would have trouble restoring order to this scene. However, using a simple technique loosely borrowed from the Native Americans, calm is restored and the situation is able to be sorted, with minimal damage.

The Faculty of Education doesn't spend a lot of time demonstrating the fine art of resolving squabbles between students. However, as you are well aware, you constantly have to don your striped jersey and act as referee in children's disputes. I'm not talking so much about breaking up physical brawls, rather the simple (to us, not them) disputes which are a part of the daytime dramas.

First, and this is vital, timing is of the essence. Teachers often feel a need to deal with issues the moment they come up. As soon as a problem arises, they pepper kids with questions, hoping for a quick

Pass the Bottle

fix so they can get on with the day. While this can have merit in some cases, I've found from long and often painful experience, that this particular now, is not usually one for talking. More often than not, kids are too upset to speak rationally after an incident. It's very difficult to get them to be flexible when they're still irate. It's also a challenge to illicit 100 per cent truth. Of course, the better you know your student, chances are you'll recognize which path to take.

Let's try a more prudent first response, one I assure you will set the right tone. "I understand that you're very upset right now. I really do want to work this out so we can all be happy again, but I think right now you need some time to calm down and think about why you're upset. Besides, the rest of the class is ready to carry on with their work. So I promise that when we have quiet time, we'll all sit down and give everyone a chance to say what they have to say." This is a rather long-winded version. The fewer words used, the better.

The results of this approach are multi-faceted. It takes some of the urgency away from the situation, so processing may be a much easier and relaxed affair. Sometimes kids might decide that what they were angry about was not so important. Often, I was told it was okay and they had it all settled, before I even had a chance to be involved. Also, the act of becoming occupied in another activity will often diffuse the situation.

Of course, there may be times when you have to separate the kids for safety safe. However, as a rule, don't try to work things out while there are still sparks flying.

When it comes to discussing the problem, my favourite practice has always been the bottle technique. It started one day when the kids were all talking over each over. We handed a water bottle to one of the kids and made a few simple rules. Only the person holding the bottle was permitted to talk. An important caveat was if he became abusive or raised his voice, he lost his chance to speak until the end. If someone interrupted, their "testimony" would also be delayed.

If you don't have a bottle you can use stuffed toys, pencil cases, or any other objects at hand. The point is, it worked. The kid with the bottle felt as if she was being heard, and the others knew they would have their say later, without the fear of insult or ridicule.

While this didn't necessarily resolve the issue on the spot, it provided space for a calm, mostly honest discussion, which brought about a speedier resolution. Often, the kids helped determine the consequences, if there were any. Please remember, there don't always have to be consequences. By having each child decide what should be done as part of the group, it was unusual for anyone to feel they were being unfairly treated. The more experienced the kids became at this process, the more seamless it became, and the less stressful for everyone involved. It also prevented that most dreadful of all penalties, the 15-minute teacher lecture.

There will always be arguments and conflicts. According to their gravity, there will be times when it may be necessary to act swiftly. In most cases though, you and your children will agree that the resolution of quarrels will keep until it can be dealt with in an orderly, fair and peaceful manner, where it's unlikely anyone will feel hard done by.

CHAPTER FORTY-THREE

When We Belittle

> If we would be activists for good, for the positive, we must assume responsibility for our minds, as well as our speech.
>
> —Robert Thurman, *Inner Revolution*

Early in my teaching career I had one very boisterous homeroom class. An assortment of large personalities can produce a lot of noise. They were particularly spirited when they were at their lockers. Like many an inexperienced teacher, I would stand there and nag them to be quicker, quieter, kinder, anything that would make my life easier.

One of my boys was bigger and looked older than the rest of the grade 6 boys. This often led teachers to expect behaviour far beyond his twelve years. He was an easy-going lad, but one day he and another student got into a minor tiff resulting in some pushing and then tears. In the process of getting it sorted, I pointed a finger at S. and said, "You're acting like a kid". He didn't take a second to reply, "But I am a kid." Sufficiently chastened, I bid a hasty retreat.

You know a funny thing happens when we belittle somebody; we actually become little. Intentionally or not, adults frequently demean children. Educators are certainly no exception. In fact, they can be among the worst culprits. In our attempt to move children along in life, we are apt to put expectations upon them that they cannot possibly reach and when they fail, we call them up on it, often in cutting and cruel ways.

As purveyors of negative epithets, grownups are prolific. When kids don't measure up to our image of perfection we act as if there's something wrong with them. We rarely consider the possibility what we are demanding is not only unrealistic, but often unnecessary. Once again, I'll ask the question posed earlier in this journey. "Is the adult behaviour children often see us display, something to which our kids should aspire?"

Go into many primary classes and watch as the teachers try to insist their children sit on their bottoms in a circle, hands folded neatly on laps. Try to comprehend why it is so important that students in higher grades put their names on the upper left or right-hand corner of the paper and underline it in a fixed manner. And who really cares if our kids are lined up in ruler straight queues, without speaking a word? Yes, I hear you argue that we need to have some kind of order and discipline to prevent chaos. While I have no argument with that, I can swear from experience, all of the great teachers I have known didn't nitpick. This relaxed attitude doesn't cause the kids to run amuck. The truth is, many of our rituals are little more than an instructor's need to be in complete control. The more rigid and numerous the rules are, the more likely you're dealing with a petty dictator of an adult, who fears, and in all likely hood doesn't even like children. Also, remember the more trivial rules you make, the more time you will spend enforcing them.

Try to recall how many times you've said, "Act your age." "You should be ashamed of yourself." "Nobody else is acting like that." Join in at any time and add your own. When a teacher dresses a child down in front of his peers two things happen. First, the child instantly has a hole shot into their self-esteem, a fragile image which may already have been peppered with adult gunfire. The second impact happens with rest of the class. Kids suddenly see your act for what it really is, a pathetic attempt on the part of a small person, to grab control and respect. In that moment, you become small as well. The dynamics which then come into play are destructive and demoralizing for everyone.

When We Belittle

As long as we remain human, there will be times when we are frustrated or angry with our kids. But these are the times when we must reach for the deeper part of our self, the part which has nothing to do with ego. If we've practiced witnessing our behaviour, becoming aware of our feelings, we'll be more likely to catch ourselves before we speak or act harshly. At that moment we may do well to simply pause and be silent. A simple look is usually enough to redirect a child without making them lose face. Many teachers have a clear signal which they use to remind kids they've stepped over the line. There are countless ways we can express ourselves without using ridicule. Take a look at what you're trying to accomplish as instructors, and redefine your priorities. Are issues being created where none need exist? Do they serve any purpose in the classroom?

This is the time in a child's life when much of their confidence is developing and adults will help paint a huge part of that picture. Every cutting comment will help deflate a child a little more. Each unreasonable expectation or useless rule we make, creates another opportunity for a child to feel they don't measure up. It also calls into question your own integrity.

Let go of the need for control. Say goodbye to the petty tyrant in you. When you are angry or frustrated, don't let your ego or pride turn you into a bully. At this point, just shut up and wait until what you say or do can be put to positive use. This much we owe to ourselves and our children.

CHAPTER FORTY-FOUR

Who Are We Really Trying to Correct?

> The teachers who get burned out are not the ones who are constantly learning, which can be exhilarating, but those who feel they must stay in control and ahead of the students at all times.
>
> —Frank Smith, *The Book of Learning and Forgetting*

A good friend of mine, sadly no longer around, had some odd instructional quirks. While his students were guaranteed to get a wide ranging academic experience, they had to endure some challenging eccentricities. J. could not just have his kids line up at the door. They had to be completely silent, standing in a razor straight line, at rapt attention. Until this was achieved, they were neither allowed into or out of the room. When there was a school trip, classes usually met outside at the nearby bus stop. It was not unusual to wait 15 minutes for his group to finally join us. It was expected. While he thought he was simply employing good management techniques, chances are his mania was driven by a need to control. I regret never really asking him why he felt this was necessary. Teachers don't like to question their colleague's methods.

Who Are We Really Trying to Correct?

Many teachers who insist on an inflexible regimen are exercising a need to dominate by acting as mini despots, lording their power over those who have no recourse. Even those of us who would never think of ourselves bullies, sometimes fall into this trap. Perhaps it's out of frustration or pressure. Whatever the reason, when we act this way, we lose our capacity to work with our kids in a positive, affective way. When too much time is spent on the details, what's really meaningful pays the price.

As you've heard before, self-awareness is the best way to prevent us falling into this trap. By stepping back from ourselves, it's as if we've actually moved out of our own body, floated across the room, plunked ourselves in an easy chair and gently watched the way that person we call "I" behaves. Ask yourself what kind of behaviour that individual is trying to correct. How do they look and sound when they are doing it?

When we have done that objectively, we're ready to dig a little deeper. Does what we're trying to alter actually need fixing in the first place? Is it crucial to the child's well-being and growth, or is it just important to us? Why do we feel such a need to change the behaviour? What are we really trying to pull off here? Is it just our fears and ego taking over? That's a pile of questions. But they need our honest consideration.

Perhaps it's misguided good intentions. The problem is, our actions are often nothing more than a mask which allows the ego to think, "Look at me, trying to help this poor child improve himself. I'm helping to turn him into a better person. Aren't I a wonderful teacher?"

Acute awareness of our actions and motivations is the gateway to helping children discover their endless capabilities and wonderful qualities. Sometimes what we do in the name of helping children grow is no more than a way of validating ourselves.

Many times, our reactions are completely knee-jerk, because we aren't paying attention. When the day is over and we have the time to relax and clear our minds, it helps to go back and recall how we behaved ourselves. Then we can see more clearly where we are coming from when we interact with the kids. The more often we do this, the better chance we have of understanding our motives. It's here we can catch ourselves before we damage those in our trust. As we practice this and start to gauge our actions and reactions, we automatically drop our pettiness and superior attitude.

Re-direction is always going to be a part of teaching. Zen masters used a stick to help their disciples come to awakening (definitely not recommended in your position). Sometimes we will need to be sharp with our students in an effort to have an impact. On occasion, we will act badly. But if we pay more attention to our actions and look more deeply into ourselves, we won't manage through force and fear, and in the end, we will operate more impeccably in each situation.

CHAPTER FORTY-FIVE

A Word About Words

> May the spirit in you move your lips and direct your tongue.
>
> —Kahlil Gibran, *The Prophet*

On a trip to Edmonton some years back, the skies became spiteful. It felt as if we were on a very old roller coaster with square wheels. I'm a pretty good flyer, but that day I gave the armrest a good bending.

Across the aisle from me was a young mother from Newfoundland, with her small infant on her lap. From the start of the trip until we arrived, this child smiled, laughed and slept. The odd time she started to get fussy, a warm word or smile from mum was enough to placate her. Between the weather and a couple of unexpected delays, the flight turned into a bit of a marathon. Yet baby remained unruffled by the events, and seemed as happy as can be. At the end of the flight, I leaned over to say something to the mother. All my years working with kids have made me hesitant to label kids as good or bad, so I said, "That's such a peaceful baby." "Yes," she replied, "She's a good baby!"

"Good" is a term we often toss around when we refer to children. We say, "You're a good boy or girl." We praise them in front of others by saying, "She really is a good kid." What's the problem, you might say? The thing is, we then are implying there is an opposite, in this case, bad. "You're very bad for doing that." Well I've never seen a bad kid. They may be fractious, even down right ornery at time, but that does not make them bad. Take stock of some of the words you use when talking to your students. Then ask yourself whether they are helping, or doing harm.

There is great power in words. With this in mind, you have to wonder why we keep telling kids they are good when they please us, and suggest they are bad when they don't. I'm not saying the word "good" is taboo, we just need to be wary of how we throw it around. Try to be more specific. Zero in on what the "good" is. "You're very helpful." "That was kind of you." "He just makes me smile all the time." By doing this, we drop this duality of good kids and bad kids. While our children may try our patience, it makes them neither good nor bad, just human.

There are two reasons words are the root of so much grief. The first involves the kind of talk which comes out of our mouths. Having covered that, let's move to number two. Most of the time, we talk too much. Think about the occasions when you've been cornered by someone who won't stop jabbering. You just want to find a magic hole and jump in, or better yet, give them a push. Adults tend to use entirely too many words with kids. The more we talk, the truth is, the less they're likely to tune in and listen. So we need to be frugal with our words. Say what we want to say and then shut up. The surest way to lose a child's attention is to ramble on and repeat what's already been said in five different ways.

Be aware that even though children may only hear a fraction of what we say, they do catch the most important bits. For this reason, it's important to choose our words wisely. You can guarantee many of the words a child takes to heart are the ones you wish we could take back.

CHAPTER FORTY-SIX

Do You Think They Really Like Me?

> Getting people to like you is really the other side of liking them.
>
> —Dr. Norman Vincent Peale,
> *The Power of Positive Thinking*

When I heard some elected officials were suggesting an incentive program for teachers I thought perhaps my ears were playing tricks on me. After letting the absurdity of the whole idea settle, an army of questions immediately followed. The first being, "Are you people serious?" Followed by, "Is something wrong with you?" After that they became a bit more concrete. With what scale would you measure this exemplary educator? Marks? Attendance? The number of pretty pictures on the walls? The quietest classroom? I'm not sure how I would answer the first two queries, but I do know the answer to the rest, "None of the above, because there is no such gauge."

I'll tell you what first class learning looks like. The classroom is a fun place to be, where kids are engaged and serious learning occurs. At first glance, the room may look a bit chaotic as students mill around their much-loved teacher, asking questions and showing off their work. Much of the time activity abounds, with kids working together tackling challenging tasks, in order to unravel meaningful problems. Students are not often found at their desks because their teacher knows real learning doesn't happen when an instructor is lecturing. Yet, when there is a need to come together to talk or receive instruction, students are well mannered, attentive and considerate of each other.

You rarely hear a raised voice from this person. When issues come up between children, they are handled promptly and judiciously. The kids in this room don't fear their teacher, and yet they would never consider being defiant or unkind. Why? I believe it comes down to a very simple principle. This teacher has a love for and understanding of kids, particularly his students. All teachers hope they will be liked by their pupils. As it turns out, as a measure of success, it holds a lot of weight. If the teacher cares deeply for his students, they in turn truly love and respect him. Did I mention test scores in all this? I guess I didn't.

As the human experience is fraught with uncertainty, somewhere deep inside people want to be liked. We come out of first meetings wondering whether we made a good impression. Teenage boys speculate whether the girl three rows over fancies them. Parents want to know how their kids really feel about them.

Yet there are teachers who still cling to the old "I'm not here to be liked" line. That's the biggest load of bunk ever invented to justify a failure to connect. Maybe these worn out, grumpy old educators will teach their students the curriculum, and the children just might absorb some of it. Perhaps they'll be compliant out of dread. However, this misses the whole point of education. The educational experience is a two-way street. The teacher brings to the students, and likewise receives from each child in his care. When that occurs, learning is happening every day, to everyone in the room.

Mind you, being liked is not a goal, and if you try, you most certainly will fail. However, despite what many will have you believe, being liked is important, simply because of what it stands for. If you are truly fond of your students, enjoying the time you share, and are committed to their welfare, you will be liked. When your program is engaging and kids look forward to the day's activities, they will love learning. If your expectations are clear, but reasonable and flexible, you will be respected. There's no secret formula for this. There is nothing you have to try to do. Your students know a caring, loving individual, and they will respond with the same. There will never be a merit system which can measure exemplary teaching, and those who suggest it have no business dabbling in education.

Only when real connection is established, can the educational experience begin in earnest. Students know your directions are given with their interests at heart, and as a result, they are willing to join you in the experience. And if one or two students haven't bought in, most likely the others will bring them around.

This directly contrasts with teachers who impose authority through tyranny and intimidation. Teachers who are rigid and don't empathize with their students may be able to enforce order. They will no doubt meet their personal goals, but in truth there is little of value going on, even if standardized test results indicate otherwise. Learning is not imposed, it is shared. The truly successful teacher employs boundaries and limits, but these will rarely be tested when students know everything you do comes from a place caring and compassion. And yes, they will like you to boot!

CHAPTER FORTY-SEVEN

Returning to The Garden

> Real education leads to the liberation of the mind.
>
> —Abhijit Naskar, *The Education Decree*

Once in a while I have the itch to make some changes. Not the life altering ones, rather a little scenery adjustment around the house. The phone is shifted to a different table, books are moved about to new shelves. These are simple tweaks, done in the interest of aesthetics, efficiency or sudden impulse. The problem is, for the next several weeks I keep heading to the TV when the phone rings, or trying to put my book onto an imaginary side table.

Generating change is somewhat like that. It's more about unlearning old patterns than initiating old ones. This is the only way to permanently alter your behaviour. You've had a lifetime to cultivate your old patterns and beliefs, so it's not likely a rash choice is going to fix everything. Just ask any gambler or smoker.

School age children are becoming inured into the myths of our society. They are brainwashed every day thanks to television, advertising, and the lifestyles of others. No matter how well-intentioned and informed parents may be, children are constantly bombarded with these common myths:

- Power is strength, strength is power: Nearly every video game and action movie teaches superior physical strength and guile equals power.
- Money buys happiness. Check it out. Force yourself to view two or three reality shows and their advertisements. Don't get up during the adverts. If you watch carefully, you'll discover happiness is a new car, a vacation, more furniture, a good meal, fast food, comfort, or winning a lottery. If that doesn't cut it, try the satisfaction of thwarting someone else's success.
- The purpose of life is to get a good education, a prestigious job, raise a family and put away enough money for old age. Don't forget to lay some aside for your funeral.

All right, some of these ideas make a bit of sense, but they tend to make children grow up wearing blinders. Those who don't manage to meet these targets, feel inadequate and unsuccessful. Children need to discover there are many roads to fulfillment, and theirs may be very different from others.

Some kids may be lucky enough to have parents who are living examples of a better way to live. We have to be aware of what our students are bringing into the classroom as they start school. Then we can help introduce them to a wider view of living. This doesn't mean attacking lifestyles to which they are accustomed, but instead, finding role models and lessons which let them know they have options.

As children become more abstract in their thinking, they're eager to challenge and discuss the world around them. While we're not looking to raise a bunch of anarchists, we are moving them out of their comfort zone, so they can see perhaps all they've been told is not the final word. By introducing children to the reality of true power, happiness and fulfillment, they will begin to see what they've been exposed to all their lives is only half true.

We have an obligation to examine many of the messages together. Advertisers are very clever. They convince children that eating at McDonalds is an essential part of growing up. Kids are made to feel that if they can't get the latest game system or phone, a call to Amnesty International is in order. No matter how many charities they support, the truth is, a corporation's goal is to sell products, and children are the most lucrative consumers. It wasn't long ago a mobile phone was a luxury. It's now not only a necessity, but needs to be constantly updated with the latest Aps.

We have the opportunity to gently point out healthy alternatives, both mentally and physically. This goes well beyond eating and exercising habits. Our well-being is interwoven into our whole outlook on life. Perhaps we need to be in less of a rush to shove every new gadget into kids' hands when they're barely old enough to push buttons. I honestly can find nothing endearing about a kid of seven or eight texting, or being glued to a video game when they're at a restaurant with their parents.

We can encourage families to find rewarding ways to spend time together without technology. Parents need to be strong enough to stop using the TV and game system as a baby-sitter, and to start celebrating time with their children. At school, we can have a *Turn off The Tech-a-Thon* as a fund-raiser.

Older students may welcome this kind of dialogue, but their patterns can drag them back to their old habits and attitudes. We need to help them get off the treadmill of obsession with the virtual world, and explore what the real one has to offer.

Changing our habits and unlearning false ideas isn't easy. The truth is buried under an avalanche of past conditioning. If we start early, our kids will wake up when they're young. Then they'll be better equipped to make their own decisions throughout life, without being manipulated by the media or their peers.

CHAPTER FORTY-EIGHT

Working with Parents

We're all in this together.

—Traditional Union Movement Slogan

When you deal with certain special needs kids you often feel like you're spinning your wheels in a deep, snowy rut. It's a test of resilience to see gains made at school being sometimes negated by what happens at home or on the street. Our efforts to inflate a sense of worth in our kids can be sabotaged by people puncturing it when we aren't looking. Then comes the awkward task of suggesting to parents that some of the things they are doing just may be sinking their kids into a deeper hole. Yet it needs to be said. So our job now becomes guiding them into changing old patterns, and hoping we can all work in the same direction.

Since students spend the other half of the day with peers and family, our best intentions are not enough if they are receiving different messages outside of the classroom. When this happens, it's one step forward and another back.

What goes on at home is largely out of our hands, but we need to make families understand what we are trying to do, so they will hopefully climb on board. Parents may not always agree 100 hundred percent with what's going on at school, but more often than not, when they clearly see everything is for the welfare of their children, and when they see their child is happy, they will co-operate. So it's essential we maintain what we are doing in the class, at home.

Parents want their kids to do well at school. So when they see what's happening is different from some of their past school experiences, they may be somewhat uneasy. For those who were schooled in a conservative, traditional way, it can be a giant leap. One thing is certain. Parents have the same concerns as you. They worry about the violence and attitudes of their kids. While they have hope for the future, they also worry their kids might follow the wrong path and end up in trouble, or may not complete their education.

When you share such common ground, it follows that if the school and the parents act together to bring children to a more self-aware, compassionate and responsible way of living, we stand a chance of affecting a meaningful change.

The unfamiliar doesn't sit well with some. At first parents may think we want to throw out all that is time honoured and familiar. They might believe we are devaluing academics and their kids won't be prepared for adulthood. We need to assure them this is not what's happening. Rather, we're moving on a path that works within the present system, but is willing to re-examine our priorities. What we're offering is a chance for a brighter future, rather than continuing something that is plainly not working.

For this to happen, we need open and direct dialogue. Parents need to be supported in nurturing the spirit of their child at home, knowing this is what's happening at school. They need to know when we make suggestions we are not questioning their competence. Instead, we're saying we can all do better. Then if we agree about this, why wouldn't we try something wise individuals and masters have proposed throughout the ages?

Parents and teachers have to be comfortable enough to meet with each other and talk about what's going on. Here, concerns can be shared and recommendations made. As with all new initiatives, they have to be part of the process and not feel as though changes are being imposed without consultation. Too often, parents are kept in the dark about policies and excluded from decision making. This should never be the case. Meetings with parents are not just for report cards and bake sales. This is all about their children and their future, and they must to be involved. Life is too precarious at this time to just carry on and leave fate to habits and patterns. It's time to have the courage to step outside our current way of thinking and explore a new and better way, together.

CHAPTER FORTY-NINE

Be as A Child

> If you carry your childhood with you, you never become older.
>
> —Tom Stoppard

When I was a kid, long before birthdays lost their sparkle, I'd be crazy with excitement as the big day approached. This wasn't only because of the presents, although I had no problem with that; but more important, I was going to be a year older. That was a big deal. All kids want to be older. Have you ever noticed every child is always going on some year? They are never nine years old; they're going on 10. We're in a hurry to grow up because the faster the years pass, the sooner we can do cool stuff like staying home alone, driving a car or seeing that restricted movie. It's a funny thing though, as those milestones come and go, something always seems to be missing. There's always another hill to climb.

Kids constantly talk about what is going to happen when they grow up. They imagine what kind of job they're going to have or where they're going to live. Maybe, they're planning on getting rich, having lots of nice clothes, or fancy cars. A huge mansion either on or beside a hill, filled with lots of kids, could be in the plan. Perhaps, they visualize their prince or princess and travelling to far and exotic places.

Dreams are fun, and a child should always be allowed to let their imaginations run to the wildest. Still, there's something sad about hearing a child, at such a wonderful stage of their life, projecting into a time when they're no longer a kid. This image isn't something they acquire on their own. As adults, we're often guilty of feeding into that way of thinking. Upon meeting a child, have you ever asked the question, "What do you want to be when you grow up?" This sort of implies they're not anybody right now.

In school, we are constantly reminding kids they are preparing themselves to ensure a bright future. While it serves everyone to inspire our children to follow their interests, we have to stop making children feel they will only be validated when they reach some lofty goal, often of our choosing, not theirs. A sign outside an elementary school near my home once proudly displayed the message, "We are here to learn and achieve and prepare for college and university." This was a middle school. Am I missing something here? Aren't there a few years to enjoy in the interim?

As adults, we seem be in a hurry to push kids to leave the innocence of childhood and get serious about life by preparing for adulthood. But childhood isn't a stepping stone. Its magic can be experienced throughout a lifetime. If as we grow older, we add wisdom, responsibility and experience to the other essences of childhood, we will be someone able to appreciate the entire spectrum of life. We'll tackle adult situations with the sobriety of an adult, but with the openness and lightness of a child.

During childhood, we are most connected to our spiritual side. Life is still available in its simplest form, and this makes us totally available. Time is not squandered, it is savoured. As adults, we know how important it is to feed the inner child, to play, taste wonder and open ourselves to the world. We need to make sure this spirit is not quenched with our dramas and personal stories.

As children grow, we can offer them our insight and life experience, but it's imperative that we truly see the wisdom of childhood, and let kids understand what they already have, rather than trying to sweep it away and replace it with our "big person" agenda.

TEACHING IN THE SPIRIT

Our kids need to see us playing, opening to our feelings and rejoicing in the miracle of life together, while also discovering the qualities they acquire through aging are another part of the dance. They will all move through time, so there's no need to hurry. In reality there is no child, there is no adult, just stages along the way. We are the same person, only dressed in different clothes. If we maintain the balance of youth and experience, we don't need to look for a better way of living. It will be right there, in each moment.

CHAPTER FIFTY

Teaching the Teacher

> When love and skill work together, expect a masterpiece.
>
> —John Ruskin

Teachers spend long hours upgrading their qualifications in the hope of getting better at what they do. Some of the workshops and courses I attended were motivating, and equipped me with skills I needed to teach more effectively. Often, I came out with a bundle of new and engaging ideas for the classroom. Other training was less inspiring.

If you already have a knack of carrying out an exciting, vibrant program with the kid's best interests at heart, PD will hopefully enhance everything you do. However, if you don't have that instinctive ability to relate to children in a caring, enthusiastic manner, you're wasting your time. In fact, adding more facts and strategies may hinder your shaky ability to relate, as you get bogged down in methodology and philosophy.

PD is an integral part in teaching the teacher. Workshops and seminars are always available in a variety of disciplines. Educators are encouraged and often required to take these courses to help them meet new standards and improve their delivery of curriculum.

Others help teachers keep pace with new technology. If your focus is special education, seminars often deal with classroom management and meeting individual learning needs.

While these have their value, a quick look over the classes offered shows something missing. There are few programs which encourage our instructors to bring a more holistic approach to either the classroom or their own lives. Courses which may offer some insight into the mind of the child, the spirit of youth and honouring the wonders of childhood, are clearly absent. Truly inspirational speakers who uplift the listener, who can rejuvenate and add life to this profession, are not usually presented. How many courses are offered to help teachers see and hear their students by practicing deep seeing and listening? The answer is to my knowledge, none. Why is that? It would mean a complete overhaul of the way we look at education and the government cannot and will not put out the money when they can't see a payoff. So they continue to teach our educators the same lessons, only wrapped in shiny new packages.

If there is no peace and balance in one's life, it's unlikely these qualities can be expressed to the children in your charge. On the other hand, if you enter the classroom feeling at ease with yourself and the world, it's possible this atmosphere will affect those around you.

Some boards of education offer workshops which give teachers the opportunity to experience wellness retreats. These are meant to encourage relaxation and balance. Mostly these are one-offs, a break from the hectic schedule and a chance to unwind. They may do some good for a short time. Inevitably, by the time teachers have been back in the grind for a few days though, it's all been for naught. What if instead, educators had ongoing sessions designed to help bring a more universal approach to their practice? Teaching such skills as practicing deep listening and meaningful dialogue could be a step towards making our classrooms more compassionate and loving places.

Our teaching philosophies tend to come from a set of traditional values and ideas which do little to advance our kids on the path to self-realization. We are currently stuck in neutral and will continue to be there, until the education system is willing to admit there's more to a good teacher than the quality of their degree, the number of courses on their resume, or the test results they deliver. By ensuring all of those in charge of our youth have access to programs which are more enlightened and focus on educating the entire child, we will help our educators bring a more open and caring aspect to their teaching. If we want to guide our children towards a more complete way of living, we should take advantage of learning from those who can guide us to be better leaders.

CHAPTER FIFTY-ONE

All We Are Saying

> Give peace a chance."
>
> —John Lennon

In 1969, John Lennon and Yoko Ono held their famous Bed-Ins in Montreal and Amsterdam. The two-week long siesta was an attempt to bring attention to the desperate need for world-wide peace. While the occasion probably did little to generate peace by itself, the ensuing media coverage played a huge part in creating a wave of peace consciousness. That decade of peace began with Martin Luther King's march on Washington and included Woodstock and many other rallies and demonstrations. While no one event brought about immediate change, these movements had a huge impact on desegregation, the collapse of the Soviet Block and the dismantling of the Berlin Wall. Sometimes the wheels of change are slow, but a critical mass of people working together can move mountains. However, the wheel needs to keep rolling for real transformation to occur.

By engaging in peace awareness in the classroom we can help keep that conviction alive for a new generation. While I wouldn't suggest having "Bed-ins" in the classroom, at least if you want to keep your job, there are many things the average teacher can do to promote individual and global harmony.

Deep down everyone wishes for peace. Children don't hesitate to convey their hopes for a more harmonious, compassionate world. Humanitarian organizations and religions throughout the world have peace at the top of their wish list. Masters, avatars and other wise men throughout history have implored us to move towards peace. They even gave us some pretty directions to follow. This all sounds like a good foundation on which to build.

Then why is this state still as elusive today, as it was in Biblical times? The answer is elemental. We're trying to make something happen in the world that many of us don't have ourselves. No matter how honourable your intentions, if your own mind and life are in turmoil, if you are not at rest with yourself, your efforts to bring about peace will fail. Even though Masters, such as Jesus, reminded us that peace is within, we've long insisted in trying to correct all our conflicts from the outside, while inside we struggle with ourselves and our relationship with life.

The true secret to a lasting peace begins with finding our own tranquillity and harmony. Sadly, few of us take time to fashion harmony in our own lives, much less help our youth to do the same. We continue to look upon peace as something which can be achieved with some sort of outside intervention. Peacekeepers dressed as soldiers try their best to enforce ceasefires in war torn areas. Countries negotiate shaky truces. But the absolute truth is, peace cannot be forced. Armistices and treaties can be imposed, but as long as the roots of violence, anger and prejudice exist, they are only band aids on open sores, which in time will fester and erupt again.

Throughout the course of history, we have seen conflicts erupt into wars, followed by uneasy ceasefires and peace talks, but the pattern is repeated over and over. Meanwhile, the solution is right at our fingertips. The seeds of peace lie within everyone, right beside the capacity for violence. It is the job of each generation to nurture these seeds, and pass them to the next. Teachers have an amazing chance to pursue this, but not many actively do. Usually the load of teaching is so onerous that the idea of peace coaching becomes another burden. Certainly, such courses are not part of the curriculum. There's just no room.

TEACHING IN THE SPIRIT

Maybe we've become too busy throwing facts at our kids. Perhaps we cling to the false idea that our leaders can lead us to peace. The truth is, kids are not being given the means to help them feel centred and still. So they end up with the same old hang-ups and illusions their parents have, which means they have little chance of truly being at ease with themselves, let alone the rest of the world. With the constant bombardment of damaging images our kids witness each day, and through the various forms of media we've addicted them to, the roots of stillness are becoming deeply buried; and not much is being done to dig them up again.

We tell children they can just walk away when others hurt or anger them. But turning the other cheek is much more than a physical reaction, it's a mind-set which comes from internal strength, and we can't expect our children to carry out this tough chore until they find themselves in a better place. That can only happen when the way they look at others and the rest of the world starts to shift.

Before we are able to help our children come to a more peaceful place, we need to start with ourselves. As adults, we can simply stop anytime during the day and bring ourselves back to presence by returning to our breathing, repeating an affirmation or stepping back and seeing our dramas for what they are. If each of us approach our day in a calm and settled manner, we will radiate a more tranquil outlook which affects everyone. Parents can use this same technique at home, in whatever fashion works for them and the family. Take some time to be silent and still and just see what a difference it makes. Remember, merely being aware of our stress begins the calming process.

Teacher Thich Nhat Han strongly advocates taking time out of our day to do simple mindfulness exercises which reinforce feelings of peace and light. In his Plum Village Retreat in France, Han says that every time the phone rings, residents stop for one moment and practice mindfulness. Perhaps we can find our own signal which will make us pause for just a moment and become aware of ourselves. That done, we move on with our day, a little more alert and mindful.

If I asked the average teacher to give five strategies to learn fractions, they could probably give 10. If the same question was asked about activities to foster inner well-being, they would likely be hard pressed to come up with one.

There are programs such as "Second Steps" which promote understanding and help our kids find empathy and compassion towards others. These are well intentioned useful programs; however, we're still stepping on to a moving train. We have to return to our starting point; coming back to what we know is really true about life.

In order to move in accord with the world, the seeds of harmony, compassion and altruism need to be recognized and nurtured.

Our first step is to help kids become more mindful in their daily lives. Brief mindfulness exercises can be practiced each day to help them get in touch with the present moment. If they are more aware of their own feelings and those of others, they'll be less likely to use hurtful words or resort to physical violence. They can learn to disagree with others; but with an appreciation of their motives. At that point they are less likely to ridicule their ideas, or lash out. Now there's a chance at a meaningful interaction, not driven by anger or the compulsion to be right. In doing this we equip children with the tools to settle differences without the need of having losers and winners.

The more we see our reflection in others, the more we recognize our own pain, hurt and anger. Then we can be more accepting of our own feelings and thoughts, instead of harbouring guilt for having them. Guilt accomplishes nothing, awareness changes everything. When we stop being violent towards ourselves, we develop more tolerance and acceptance toward those with whom we are dealing.

As we're reminded constantly, much of what children see on TV and the majority of the games they play, involves the use of force or violence to overcome adversity. In that world, power is something wielded over others to reach our goals. This is why it's so important we show children that peace is not equated with weakness. The genuine examples of power shown by men of peace are evident in the lives of such people as Martin Luther King, Nelson Mandela or Gandhi. When we expose our kids to the lives these great leaders lived, they can clearly see how powerful a force peace is. They are able to appreciate how these people changed the world without the need for brute force or violence.

In the classroom we might stop in the middle of an activity and go through some peace exercises for a couple of minutes. The value of the time we take to centre ourselves, follow the breath and maybe assert positive statements cannot be measured. With each affirmation we nurture the seeds of peace in ourselves and our children. Unlike an assignment, this isn't an exercise the kids are doing for us. This is an activity we are pursuing together, and the results will be seen not only in each individual, but in the change of energy in the classroom and the rest of the school.

Sometimes a contagion of violence can erupt when people feel lost in their anger, hurt and sense of isolation. This aggression feeds on itself until it poisons a school, community or on a larger scale, a nation. In the same manner, when we help the seeds of peace grow in each child, a new wave starts to flood the population. A surge of goodwill, confidence and compassion wells up which will not only inspire our schools, but spill over into our homes and neighbourhoods. That's one happy epidemic.

If you really question the possibility of changing the world one person at a time, reflect on this. For thousands of years humankind has tried to find peace through conflict, détente, negotiation, treaties, brute force, war, prayer, religious campaigns and peace-making organizations such as the UN. And where are we left? We're a world still awash in bloodshed, conflict or hostility. As John Lennon wrote, "All we are saying, is give peace a chance." That starts with each of us, one at a time.

The Peace Room

> When this old world starts getting me down, I go up where the air is fresh and sweet.
>
> —The Drifters, *Up on the Roof*

Imagine you're stuck in traffic in rush hour afternoon. You've had a long day at work, where things bordered on the manic. As the traffic begins to slowly move, the person behind you objects to the fact you haven't inched forward as fast as he would like. He leans on his horn and gives you a rude gesture. In the effort to act civilly, you relive your last vacation, walking through a forest of cool green evergreens, listening to the rustling pine leaves, and the songs of birds. What would you give for just five minutes of that right now?

Adults and children all need somewhere to go when they feel life is getting to be too much. Sometimes we just need to remove ourselves so we can restore order and shift back into neutral.

One thing is certain; if we are in a tense situation, and if either the circumstances don't change, or we can't remove ourselves, even temporarily, something will have to give. At this point our stress may switch to overload and our reactions can become less than skilful. They might be something we'll later regret. A long walk is probably the best prescription for relieving stress. Some people fish or golf; others do yoga.

So what happens to a child who finds he can no longer cope with what's going on in the classroom? What about the kid who has just fought 10 rounds with her family before going out the door in the morning and now has to deal with the commotion and pressures of life in the schoolyard and the classroom? While some kids are very adaptable and able to switch off their anxieties, which isn't always such a good thing, others are cannons, primed and ready for a spark to ignite them. What kids don't need at a time like this is some adult calling them on the carpet because they are distracted or disruptive. This child is trapped. They can't just pick up and go for a walk.

What is needed is somewhere kids in crisis can go to, where they feel safe, and are able to get away from the added strain of being surrounded by a demanding teacher and some thirty-odd exuberant and largely unsympathetic classmates. We're not talking about going to the principal's office for a talk, although I've known some very empathetic and loving headmasters in my time. What schools ought to have is a place I call a "Peace Room".

This might little more than a small office or stock room, with a few large pillows and soothing décor; a place conducive to defusing high-running emotions, favourable to a return to balance. Here, children feel safe and secure in the knowledge no-one is going to ask them to speak or explain anything until they are ready. If they have nothing to say in the end, that's okay. Too many times we insist kids spill their guts when that's the last thing they're ready to do. Just because we want to know, doesn't mean they're ready to talk. It's enough for them to know, when and if they're ready, they will have an attentive and sympathetic ear.

    Let's be clear. This isn't the traditional time out room where kids throw things around to get the anger out of their system. It's also not a holding cell for children who are out of control. As teachers, we have the experience to deal with those who are having issues, and if we truly see our kids, we know them well enough to determine when there is a need for a child to get away for a while, and when things can be dealt with differently. The very name, "Peace Room", explains what this room is all about. Of course, there needs to be some sort of supervision, and staff is usually hard pressed, but there are all kinds of volunteers who would be more than willing to take on such a role. Administrators may argue there is no money for such frills. It comes down to priorities. After all, what is more important than our children's mental health?

    This is a new way of looking at things, but now more than ever, it's what many kids need. When we're more aware, our exchanges with our children take on a new dynamic, and our fears of trying something fresh and innovative fall away.

What's so funny about peace, love and understanding?

—Elvis Costello

CHAPTER FIFTY-TWO

A Word About ADD And ADHD

> Beware of over focused farmers who want to set the rules and define the game.
>
> —Thom Hartmann, *Beyond ADD*

I'm a *South Park* fan because I love the way it makes us look at ourselves. Of course, many people are uncomfortable when confronted with a mirror. One episode made me sit up and say, "Right on!" It dealt with the issue of ADD and ADHD, and its humour is sadly relevant. In this episode, several of the children in the town were suspected of being ADD because they couldn't sit through all the boring, blathering lectures of their teacher. In order to test them, the kids were required to listen attentively while being read a Charles Dickens novel. Of course, like most of us, they couldn't, and as a result, every juvenile in *South Park* was immediately prescribed Ritalin. Teachers should watch this before complaining about their kid's inability to sit for long periods of time.

At this point, it's not my intent to explore this topic or offer plans of action to deal with children with ADD or ADHD. Those can be found in other books written by those with more knowledge and experience on the subject than I. However, if we are going to teach the whole child, we have to be more aware that many children just don't fit in to the system as it exists. Children with ADD and ADHD find it very difficult to live up to the expectations of the average classroom. They aren't capable of staying put for long periods of time. They need to get up and move around. After a short period, they get restless and distracted and might act out from their frustration.

Restless children have been the bane of teachers throughout the history of formal education. It's only recently that ADD and ADHD have been recognized as medical conditions. The problem is, the term medical condition is just one step away from being labelled a disease, and the simplest way to treat an illness is to prescribe medication. So now it is fashionable to give meds to help children and even adults, meet the demands of school, work, or home. While there are cases where medication may have some merit, increasing numbers of children with mild attention deficits are receiving regular doses of pills so they can fit into the system. It all sounds a little bit Orwellian to me. You aren't able to function according to the structure, so it's calm down pills for you. Perhaps, we need to stop trying to change the kids to match the keyhole, and instead adjust the keyhole itself.

There are numerous books available which give alternative courses of action for parents, such as changes in diet, physical activities and limiting electronic stimulation. Also, teachers can learn how to make it easier for a child with ADD or ADHD to not only cope, but thrive in the classroom. In most cases, awareness and empathy on the part of the instructor combined with some adjustments to the program, can make a world of difference. We have to understand that children with ADD or ADHD may be predisposed to pursuing wonderful, creative directions in life for which others in the "mainstream" are not suited, and the onus is on us to help them discover their particular gifts.

For a complete discussion of ADD and ADHD and helping children, parents and teachers to work together, I suggest the following three books by Thom Hartmann.

- Hartmann, Thom *ADD Success Stories*. Grass Valley, California: Underwood Books, 1996
- Hartmann, Thom *Attention Deficit Disorder: A Different Perception*. Grass Valley, California: Underwood Books, 1996

A Word About ADD And ADHD

- Hartmann, Thom *Beyond ADD*. Grass Valley, California: Underwood Books' 1996

Also, I would recommend:

- Weintraub, Skye *Natural Treatments for ADD and Hyperactivity*. Pleasant Grove, Utah Woodland Publishing, 1997

While we're thinking in this way, consider this. Our kids are expected to sit for extended periods, often listening to their teacher or performing seatwork, particularly in the higher grades. Physical activity in schools has been reduced to a minimum. This is all a recipe for trouble. Stimulation and motivation largely depend on the personality of the individual teacher. In some cases, these may be lacking. As educators, we all need to step back and look at our program and decide whether we are providing inspiration and excitement in the classroom, or if we're just doling out information and insisting that kids show interest. Take an honest look at what you're offering in the class, and see what you can do ignite the spark of learning and turn it into a fire.

CHAPTER FIFTY-THREE

Freeing the Arts

> Knowledge can be communicated, but not wisdom.
>
> —Herman Hesse, *Siddhartha*

Students will:
- "recognize that a unison consists of two notes on the same line or in the same space that are to be sung or played simultaneously."
- "describe how a variety of artists working in different styles and media and in different historical periods have used the elements of design and /or tools, materials, and techniques of their art (e.g. describe buildings made in different historical periods, such as the CN tower, a Native longhouse, and the Parliament buildings in Ottawa), to show how the availability of certain materials influenced the designers or architects."
- "combine locomotion/ traveling skills in repeatable sequences, incorporating a variety of speeds and levels (e.g. in novelty dances, co-operative games);

Do these look like they might be among the expectations for the University of the Arts? In fact, they are taken from the Ontario Ministry of Education Curriculum, Level Four. That is, Grade Four!

They can be found in respectively, the music, creative arts and physical education sections. If that's not enough, please note these are only part of a ponderous list of between nine and 24 similar length requirements for these subjects. That's just for one grade.

Those are a lot of words! Here's something to consider. If you bothered to read through the lofty and often byzantine language of this document, you'd find many of the words we associate with the Arts are noticeably absent. In particular, the words *enjoyment, joy, freedom, imagination, vision, inspiration, fun, free expression, non-conformity, laughter, humour,* and *wonder,* are nowhere to be found.

Mind you, to make up for it, there are lots of other words and phrases such as *demonstrate, describe, relate, understand, identify, provide support, explain, evaluate, interpret, write, memorize, technology, produce, effective use of.* Notice the pattern?

The first list is what childhood needs to be all about; discovery and wonder. The latter reads more like the words a boss would be throwing at a prospective employee for a large bank. They mark the difference between the creative and clinical. Sadly, it's the first list which carries the most weight in education today. The other is just a list of frills.

Educators have certain concepts they must teach, and so even with the most creative arts lesson, there is some kind of skill being delivered to the kids. Fair enough, but when we clog their learning with everything quantitative, imagination and free thinking become stifled.

Vision and creativity come from the heart, not a textbook. Their sources are dreams, emotion and lust for life. You can analyse and critique them ad nauseam, as they often are, but truly inspired works are meant to be savoured and felt through our entire being. A dance sometimes needs to be just that, a dance. Start to pull it to pieces and examine it, and it becomes just another drill. Sometimes a song is only a song, not a particular form of composition. Much of the time, playing is playing, with no goal except to make friends and have fun. I am always mystified that some administrators find it necessary to ask kindergarten students engaged in play, to explain what they are learning. You have to wonder what kinds of sad, stunted minds have devised this kind of direction.

TEACHING IN THE SPIRIT

Exposure to the Arts is a wonderful gift, but with the demands from administration, teachers feel afraid to have an art period where children can paint, draw or fashion anything they can imagine, for fear of being admonished for not teaching a specific skill. When skills are the sole motivation for Art, there's little time for students to be innovative, because they are too busy trying to please the teacher, in order to score a good mark. There is no time to explore making music if we're busy identifying the rhythm of a score. Poetry must be cinquain, limerick or haiku. Our drama lesson today will be to produce a tableau, because we need to fill in a rubric for the report card.

Like the Arts, Physical Education has been reduced to the acquisition of program competencies. Granted everyone needs to learn rules and skills to play team sports properly. However, when objectives and requirements become the driving force behind physical education and creative arts, these subjects choke in their own clutter of goals. Teachers struggle through one of their 40-minute, two or three per week gym sessions, trying to be sure all of the kids have been marked on their dribbling, passing and shooting. Meanwhile, the other kids are standing, waiting in line to be tested. Finally, when there are five minutes left in the period, maybe there's time for what the kids wanted and needed all along, a game.

It seems the people who wrote these expectations, either miraculously bypassed childhood, or chose to deny the entire experience. The fact that the entire list of words stated earlier in this chapter does not appear in the expectations, shows a complete lack of understanding of the point of art or physical activities. When reports go home many parents haven't the vaguest notion of what the kids are doing, because the meaning is obscured by jargon. Some just look to see if it is an "A" or "B" and don't even read the comments. But there they are, because if teachers haven't filled up a dozen lines to describe the Arts and Drama, they've not done their job.

Wouldn't you be thrilled if your child's report read: "Susie has enjoyed the music program. She loves to sing and dance with her friends. Susie has a passion for sampling all of the instruments and creating her own pieces of music. When we play selections for musical appreciation, you can see the happiness it brings her."

Guidelines are needed, but their magnitude and scope is not only unreasonable, it hampers our ability to foster inspiration in youth at a time when it is starting to develop. Somewhere, this manic quest for quantity needs to shift to make room for creativity, imagination and vision. It doesn't take a sage to realize the importance of nurturing a new generation of innovative thinkers. One thing is certain, creative and inspired learners are given little chance to reach their potential in the system as it currently stands.

In the meantime, as teachers, we must do our best to bring inventive and original approaches to the programs we are mandated to teach. Everyone is not going to major in Music or Art and Drama. If they do, then in higher grades some of the expectations of the public school curriculum may hold them in good stead.

Meanwhile, remember what a reward the Arts have to offer to our children. Don't allow the system to quench the flames of creativity before they have a chance to burn.

CHAPTER FIFTY-FOUR

Enough Already

> Those who seek the truth by means of intellect, get further and further from it.
>
> —Huang Po

One day when my niece was in Grade Four, she came home from school with a larger than usual load of homework assignments. At one point she burst into tears of frustration and asked, "Why do we have to learn all this stuff?" She was a very bright girl who did well at school. She was also artistic and creative enough to see the absurdity of what was little more than busy work.

While curriculum is needed for students to build on the skills learned each year, one look at the growing expectations shows it has become the master of the teaching profession. Courses are constantly revised in an attempt to squeeze more information into children's minds, at increasingly younger ages. Math concepts previously covered at high school levels are now thrust upon students in grades six and seven. Primary kids struggle with ideas often beyond their cognitive skills. Learning academies reap the benefits of a more advanced curriculum by tutoring students who are unable to keep up.

Enough Already

At this point we have to ask, "What's the rush?" What do we hope to accomplish by loading the curriculum with more expectations every year, at a time when children should be exploring and discovering their world? Students are obliged to master advanced skills at a time when they are just starting to discover who they are. Clearly the message many kids get from this is that self-worth is reflected in what you can do, not who you are. Kids are astute and they quickly realize when they don't measure up to others. Over time this erodes their sense of value.

This leviathan called curriculum tears at a child's self-esteem, while handcuffing teachers. Remember, teachers are required to cover the entire program, and if they don't, then they like their students simply aren't making the cut.

Documents get thicker and longer, as education officials push for children to learn more. Don't be duped into thinking this is quality of learning. This is cramming, and it serves neither the children nor their teachers. In higher grades, units of work previously contained over an entire year are now squeezed into a semester, and are expected to be covered thoroughly. Standardized tests are the touchstone of not only the student, but the teacher, the school and the principal.

The media and the politicians are among the worst culprits in this assault on our youth. Headlines scream out when our schools don't meet standards, and they sermonize that we are failing our children. What is troubling is society believes them. Administrators will do anything to reach the bar. Requirements are accepted without question, when instead, the public should be demanding to know how these benchmarks are determined, and their value to a child's growth.

Workshops and seminars instruct teachers to improve results, sometimes to the point of encouraging them to teach exclusively to the standardized tests, so their results reflect well on the administration and placate parents and the media.

This obsession with quantity is eating away at the areas where students have a chance to develop their artistic and physical gifts. Cooking and family skills are hard to find in many schools. Shop, or design and technology, is either non-existent or reduced to computer graphic work, except in Technical Schools. Schools sell their musical instruments and trim music programs to a single period a week. Likewise, arts and drama can be as little as 40 minutes a week; and physical education, two or three classes.

It's quite common to see primary and junior teachers skipping art and gym classes, in order to complete academics. All this pressure is felt by the administrators and teachers, and eventually comes to rest on the shoulders of students, where they should they should never be placed.

In ancient Roman and Greek times, school was a place where youth learned not only academics, but about life values, philosophy, arts and music. Education was not just about academic instruction. It mirrored life and wasn't separate from what went on outside. It's time to take an honest look at our schools and admit the current curriculum serves no one. We can start by education the parents, who have been largely deluded into believing that more is better. This misconception is not easy to remove. A shift will only happen when we switch our purpose of education to one that guides our children on the path of self–awareness and discovery.

How about starting with the view that childhood is sacred, not something to be shaken out of children on the way to adulthood. Learning is meant to be a joyful journey. Each new piece of knowledge is to be explored and pondered, not just used a stepping stone for more information. This message needs to reach those in charge, who seem to have lost all perspective. Teachers must speak up. Instead of constantly revising the curriculum, we need to reconsider the object for learning. Sometimes less is better.

There are many private and alternative schools which embody these views. A large number of parents are opting to send their children to schools where they know they will receive an experience which nurtures both body and spirit.

Waldorf Schools, which currently number about 600 worldwide, have a philosophy based on honouring and protecting the wonder of childhood. Children are encouraged to be free thinkers and explore their creativity. Curriculum does not cater to government and economic demands. Imagination is nurtured and there is less emphasis on academics during the earliest years.

Subjects are taught in depth and looked at through different perspectives, so that students acquire more insight and depth. Art, music and even gardening are central to the curriculum.

Proponents of our current structure argue this kind of education won't equip a child for the real world. Education is not solely about preparing a child for adult life, any more than preparing a meal is just about sitting down to eat. Life is about discovering each moment, not just reaching a goal. When caring educators and balanced programming meet, children will be able to pursue a path at which they will not only excel, but will bring them joy in their adult years.

While most parents can't afford to send their children to alternative schools, if they are willing, educators and innovators can learn from them and open to their philosophies, while adapting them to our own public system.

Many of the ideas central to alternative schools could create tremendous, positive changes in the public system, and contrary to what we are told, they would not cause society to crumble into ruins.

By conceding that curriculum is too large to be taught effectively, our style of learning can become less urgent, less neurotic. Real educators need to have input into the development of curriculum, as opposed to so called experts, who clearly have no idea what balanced learning is all about. This puts less pressure on both teachers and students. Physical Education and the Arts can once again become a meaningful part of the program. Special options and activities can be offered which peak the interests of children. It may be here a child discovers a passion in a school system which had previously been a discouraging and uninspiring place.

Instructors who are more relaxed and working in tractable circumstances will be better teachers, effective mentors and inspiring role models. This will infect the entire school character, creating a new and exciting environment. Without balance in the education system, we pass our own hang-ups onto our children. With a new vision of education, we can take some time to smell the roses, and even grow them.

CHAPTER FIFTY-FIVE

Thank You for The Music

Make a joyous noise unto the Lord.

—Psalm 100:1

The Pied Piper of Hamlin had it all figured out. He knew music has the magical power to heal. So when the local folk ran out of solutions to rid themselves of a rat problem, they called him in. By playing his beautiful songs, the rats became so enchanted they followed him out of the town and never returned. Nice concept!

Music is a gift from the universe. It's inspired humankind throughout history. It has the power to motivate. Music connects people to peace and truth. Its therapeutic qualities are proven for both humans, animals and even plants. It can induce a state of meditation and mysticism. A heart that has experienced pain can be soothed by the right song. The right chord can break a heart wide open. It inspires its closest cousin dance, to bring us back to our ancient roots. Music runs deep in our blood and flows through our field.

Kids instinctively love music. Everything in our children calls out to experience its gifts. Music and dance can define a culture, which is why many immigrants have ensured their children grow up knowing their musical cultural background. Our musical heritage is literally in our DNA. Spirituality and music are inseparable. Without it, we lose a part of our essence.

Then why is it when the education budget is trimmed, music is one of the first subjects to feel the pinch? In the past couple of centuries, music has gone from being a cornerstone of education to almost a complete throwaway. This is probably because music has no tangible value in our business and economy based society. To get ahead in the corporate and professional community you need math, science and language. Above all, it's technology which makes the machines of business run. Music is nice, but it doesn't turn the wheels of commerce. What parent is happy when their child announces they want to be a performer? Producing artistic individuals is not the mandate of the public education system. If a kid is going pursue music as a career, let her take lessons on her own time, with her own money. After all, how many kids will grow up to be musicians?

So for the most part, music has been pushed to the back of the classroom. It starts out nicely enough in kindergarten. Teachers give the kids all kinds of instruments they can shake and bang. Children sit around in circles creating sounds with their drums, bells, cymbals, tambourines and Orff instruments. It has a lot of promise. Then a funny thing happens as children move up through the grades. Academics move to the forefront and push everything else onto the back burner. Teachers struggle to keep up. Schools scramble to find enough money for textbooks and the latest technology. Something has to go. That's usually the arts.

Not many teachers of classes in the junior and older grades give music more than a token gesture. Many teachers lack the confidence to deliver more than a superficial coverage, often little more than the rendering of a traditional folksongs or a popular Disney tune; perhaps an occasional recorder session. Some districts are fortunate enough to have an itinerant specialist who visits schools on a regular basis. However, that's rarely more than a 45-minute period, once a week, and when it's over, the classroom teacher considers himself fortunate to be done with it for another cycle.

Higher grades may have a permanent music teacher, but the number of classes is limited, and sometimes music is semestered with art, so it only lasts half a year.

Certain secondary schools feature comprehensive programs which include bands, string sections, choirs and lavish musical productions, but for the most part there is neither time nor money to permit such extravagance. If you have your heart set on pursuing music in the higher grades, better attend a School for The Arts.

This all sounds a bit grim, but there's a lot you can do without enrolling in a music course, and you needn't be particularly talented or knowledgeable to run a meaningful program, using some innovative ideas.

One of the most rewarding forms of music is to go back to the kindergarten model and fashion it around the Drum Circle. Drum circles are a sacred base for many societies and religions, and they can bring a wonderful sense of community to the class room. This can be extended by exploring the drumming traditions of various cultures.

Students in a drumming circle undergo a remarkable marvelous new experience. Suddenly they are truly working together as a team, part of a larger whole. They don't feel inferior or centered out, because this is a group effort with no real script. The rhythm and the music take themselves wherever they go. For once, there is little need for the teacher to be directing and giving instructions. A drumming circle has its own motion. Unlike singing in the choir, drumming and clapping require no real aptitude. As the individual feels he or she is becoming part of the troupe, their natural sense of timing and beat start to drive the ship. Drumming and clapping circles become magical places where everyone can experience success and belonging. The comradeship that is developed among class mates is transformational. It can take place at any time during the day. Whenever the mood feels right, you can make it happen. It also doesn't cost much and if real drums are out of the question, coffee cans and home-made maracas can do the trick. Have I sold you yet?

Another marvelous way to explore our traditions is through chanting. Many drama teachers use chanting as a means of teaching synchronized poetry readings. Chanting can begin simply as learning the alphabet or months of the year in early grades, to reciting poems and messages as children get older. During later grades, when students use chants as part of the music program, teachers can find videos of various ethnic and sacred ceremonies and involve the children in experimenting with these. Despite whatever doubts may be running through your mind, let me assure you children love chants, and if you start them young, the enthusiasm is likely to last through the years.

Chanting and drumming form a seamless segue into the themes of dance and drama. Children can re-create some of the legends of Native North Americans, African roots, or explore their personal musical heritage.

In early grades, there's no real need to have children read notes and identify and employ standard rhythms. Don't destroy the magic by introducing the mechanics of music or dance too soon. That just creates a barrier to joy and openness, and turns it into just one more tedious subject to be tolerated, rather than experienced.

Music can and must be brought back into the classroom in a way which is meaningful to children. Music and dance are a part of who we are. It's time to remember this integral part of ourselves, and how it brings us into harmony with the whole of life and each other.

CHAPTER FIFTY-SIX

Opening Up the Field

> Arrogance is one of the things that education certainly doesn't counteract, it actually favours.
>
> —Rupert Sheldrake, *Natural Grace*

On a trip to the library some time ago, I was ferreting through the shelves for something new to read. Sometimes a title is all it takes to pull me in. There it was; *Natural Grace*. The liner notes promised an upbeat dialogue between two brilliant authors, whose individual works I had previously enjoyed. I looked forward to going home and pouring a nice glass of something to compliment a good evening's read.

One half of the conversation was Matthew Fox, an Episcopal priest who has long attempted to reconcile traditional Christian thinking with a more metaphysical view of the universe. His iconoclastic pursuit of stripping religion to its most elemental, has long rankled the Catholic Church.

The other voice belongs to Rupert Sheldrake, the director of Studies in Biochemistry and Cell Biology at Clare College in Cambridge. He is most renowned for his theories of morphic resonance; simply put, the collective memory of all species which exists across time and space. This dialogue between science and spirituality is a concept woefully absent in modern education.

As I browsed through the table of contents, the seventh chapter leaped from the page. "Revitalizing Education." Surely these two ground breaking scholars would offer fresh ideas on the subject. I resisted the urge to read it in the car.

Safely seated on my couch, I thumbed through aforementioned chapter and was not disappointed. Here was so much of what I was trying to say, being said so succinctly. If this idea resonates, I strongly urge you to pick up the book. I guarantee, you will find progressive ideas which can bring freshness into your both your thinking and teaching.

At the heart of the discourse is the assertion that there needs to be a basic paradigm shift for any change to occur in the current world situation. This shift has to start with children. The trouble is education keeps using the same old template. As learning is of paramount importance to our children's future, logically, education must be at the vanguard of any change. Those we hold in trust to our youth need to open their eyes, and unlock their minds so education can be re-created.

One of the biggest laments of both men is that virtually all spirituality, with the exception a token nod to some basic character education, has been separated or removed from the school agenda. This comes partly from the fear that adding this to the curriculum may be branded as religion. Add to this the concern that including a nod to any form of faith, results in others feeling excluded. So we do what is safe and chuck out anything which deals with the numinous.

Meanwhile, our kids, through their addiction to the media and the materialism around them, receive a false set of values about life. By carrying on with our outmoded view of teaching, we deny them the wonder an all-encompassing approach to learning can provide.

Sheldrake and Fox don't advocate taking religion into the schools, or preaching spiritual beliefs to kids. Rather, they are suggesting that an exposure to a wealth of cultures and religions offers a richness of art, culture, dance, chanting and other creative channels, all of which can help open the imagination and the spirit. Sadly, all of these are being crushed by the modern world around us.

TEACHING IN THE SPIRIT

Information and technology are wonderful tools to explore the wonders of our world. However, the richness of that world is largely ignored when we narrow our teaching solely to academics and equate factual knowledge with wisdom.

This amazing chapter features creative suggestions for revitalizing our studies of science, social studies and the arts; ideas which incorporate customs and cultures from around the world and throughout history. Many of these have been already employed to rave reviews in schools all over the western world from the critics who truly count, the students. When we open our children to a new way of looking at the world, we take nothing away from their learning, and put true meaning back into education. Instructors can be free to encourage kids to explore and experience the universe with all her wonders, without fear of excision from administrators.

As classroom teachers, we have the experience to know how we can bring interesting and creative readings into our language program. We can let children explore ideas which truly interest them, stimulate their curiosity, and promote their imagination, all within the expected parameters and established procedures of the current system. New directives need to be created by open minded, insightful individuals rather than conservative planners who pedal what is safe learning, based on fear of reproach. By exploring more of the esoteric and thought-provoking works, we can help motivate and expand our kid's universe.

Teachers need to feel comfortable exploring new avenues of education, without the constant concern of meeting quotas or being reprimanded. The school years offer the marvelous opportunity to be completely remarkable, rather than settling for mediocrity. Education has so much to offer our kids and we owe it to them to have the courage, imagination and energy, to see they experience all they can.

CHAPTER FIFTY-SEVEN

The Living World

> The Universe begins to look more like a great thought, than a great machine.
>
> —Sir James Jeans, *The Mysterious Universe*

Sometime early in childhood we learn an oak tree grows from an acorn. Academically, this is easy to explain and understand. Considering that, did you ever step back from this scholarly perspective and truly consider the wonder of a tree? A simple acorn, which can become a squirrel's supper, contains all the data to one day produce a magnificent tree 10 metres high. When you look more deeply, this isn't just science, it's a miracle of existence, one too often overlooked.

One of the reasons the spark of life leaves many of us in childhood, is our casual approach to this world. Wonder is at our doorstep, but in our need to explain everything, we overlook the marvels of the universe.

While scientific knowledge has grown by leaps and bounds, our drive for answers has taken us away from what was once a vibrant, living view of the world and the cosmos. What aboriginal people have always known, we are just starting to rediscover. The people we called Pagans lived their lives in tune with nature. Somewhere between the Renaissance and the time of Newton, the cosmos took on a new, but very rigid structure which may or may not have had a creator, who designed the cosmos, set things in motion, and moved on to bigger affairs.

Not to knock Newton. He was a pretty clever fellow. However, it's the Newtonian view of nature which largely started us on the path of separation from creation. Newton explained how the universe works in the same way a factory guide would explain the machinery used to build a car. The rules of the cosmos were set in motion, and were fixed and immutable.

The problem is, when all the questions are answered and mysteries reduced to facts, the magic gets lost in the mix. This cold, mechanical view of our world has also driven us to the edge of an ecological abyss.

The idea that science is somehow separate from us leads to a host of wrong assumptions. The notion that nature and man are separate, relieved us of any responsibility of caring for the Earth. Now, when we talk about saving the planet, it's with panic and fear.

No matter how well intentioned we are, when we teach kids this way, we miss the mark. The Universe and the Earth are not fixed and unchanging. They don't exist apart from us. We aren't spectators viewing this factory called Earth, but part of the living, dynamic ever-changing wonder of this universe. The Earth, and the laws it seems to go by, are always in motion. Evolution isn't a theory, but a living reality. Creation wasn't a one-off, it's a constant process.

This doesn't mean we have to trash all we have learned. Our discoveries have been an integral part of this dynamic system. But we need to teach science in a less dogmatic manner. Gravity indeed makes an apple fall, but the fact that existence is constantly reworking itself also means we can create a rocket ship which escapes Earth's pull and heads for the stars. Quantum physics shows objects can being two places at the same time. Do we truly know what an animal or plant senses or feels?

If we can overcome this superior attitude of being the lords and masters of this planet and break free of our need to have everything figured out and put into neat little classes; then we'll be able to open to a very big idea indeed. We really don't know everything. The truth is, there's no need to know it all. So with this in mind, we don't throw out the science we are teaching, but we look at our knowledge of science from a much more humble stand point. We acknowledge the ancients and Aboriginals were on to something much larger, which we in our sense of self-importance, have rejected throughout the years. That larger something is that evolution is a constant process of innovation. Intelligence is imbued in every part of this universe.

Our science and geography texts need to reflect this vision. The views of the Industrial Revolution shaped are as worn out as the factories which have survived them. It's time to open our minds enough to realize the wonders of this amazing world.

Looking at science as a creative endeavour, rather than a static machine presents us with limitless and exciting ways of teaching. It becomes a journey, where both instructor and student see the world opening up before them, where questions have no boundaries, and not having an answer is a spring board for discovery.

Most importantly, we can once again cross the chasm our old science created. It is no longer us and science. There is no division. When we look at life through these eyes, we allow ourselves to once again stare at the heavens in wonder and awe. We can smile in gratitude when we see the buds opening in the springtime, and marvel at the workings of an ant colony. Every time we look around us we can be amazed at the way our eyes work. Then we can step back from our purely academic views of nature, and watch creative intelligence unfold.

> Everything is amazing, and no-one is happy.
>
> —T-shirt slogan in Kensington Market, Toronto

CHAPTER FIFTY-EIGHT

For the Love of The Mother

> We do not inherit the Earth from our ancestors, we borrow it from our children.
>
> —Native American Proverb

The Day the Earth Caught Fire was a 1950's B science fiction movie, now considered a touchstone for ecological disaster movies which have followed. It dealt with the staggering effects of nuclear testing on the Earth's climate. This may have been the first film in which made humankind was made culpable for its careless actions. It also illustrated how we directly affect the whole of nature. Although it is now considered a classic, its message was largely ignored and it was deemed little more than a good action film at the time. Later offerings such as *The Day After Tomorrow* and Al Gore's *An Inconvenient Truth*, triggered increasing numbers of people to wake up and take notice of the way our activities are manifested in the ecological chaos around us.

The Earth is our mother. She supports all life as we know it. From the single celled life forms, to the most complex of animals, the thread of life is interlocked with the heart of the planet. This is Gaia, the living Earth. In ancient times, humankind believed it their duty to honour and protect her. Then, from the industrial age on we raped and pillaged her, giving nothing back. Now, our Mother is in a state of distress, made more apparent by the incidence of natural disasters and the ominous spectre of potentially catastrophic climate change.

Into the latter part of the last century, our lessons mirrored this careless and ungrateful attitude. We studied the Earth in terms of available resources and how they benefit the world's economy. Gross national product, export and import data all seemed terribly important to my Geography teachers. The study of the Sciences did nothing to make us see the Earth as our living partner in the journey of creation. It was something we lived on, had complete dominion over.

Over the past decades there has been a shift in the way we look at planet Earth. Environmentalists have implored us to examine the reckless way we've been living. Irrefutable evidence about climate change and impending global calamity stare us in the face. Finally, we are starting to re-examine the wisdom of our Native ancestors, who have always been aware of our-inter being with all life. Governments have slowly come to admit we need a new paradigm in our attitude towards our home. Legislation to protect our planet and all its living brothers and sisters is beginning to shed a ray of hope for our future. Of course, political wrangling and corporate clout threaten to delay action when it is most needed, with North American nations lagging behind the much of the world.

Eminent scientists are starting to see the world as a living entity, rather than an ancient rock which fortuitously sprouted life. In the schools, our outdated textbooks are being amended to reflect this new respect and reverence for our Mother. However, we still are poised at the edge. The world is at the boundary, between a complete collapse into entropy, or a new age, where humankind finally starts to realize its place in nature and stops acting as lord and ruler of the universe.

Our children hold the key. At this crucial fork in time, there is no choice but to press forward in teaching our children the truth about our home. This goes much deeper than simple eco awareness. Our complete attention needs to turn to how we can once again start living in harmony with our world. This means also looking seriously about our culture of rampant consumerism.

It's no time for baby steps. We need to be all in with our commitment. We can begin by looking at examples and stories of how Aboriginal people, world-wide, have lived their entire history in complete accord with their surroundings. Our next step is take kids out of the classroom and into nature so they can appreciate its wonder. We can help our kids see how all those products they are convinced they need are exhausting the Earth's resources.

From there, kids can take the lead. Schools can band together in projects which help clean up the community. We have to power to motivate our neighbourhoods. Our students are responsible enough to educate their parents in all things environmental.

Our negligent attitude towards our planet is not something we're born with. It's something we learn. If we can be taught to disrespect the Earth, we can rediscover how to respect her,

When we study the features of the Earth, we can go far beyond the facts and statistics, looking at their beauty, how they affect the whole planet and what can be done to keep them alive and undefiled. Textbooks need to be updated so they not only stress the facts, but also give insight into the wonder and magic of life itself. Science and Social Studies must move beyond the classroom and into the natural world. If children grow up with a feeling of wonder and reverence towards our Mother Earth, they will also hold a sense of responsibility towards their home. We don't have the luxury of only being concerned with what falls directly on our doorstep. We are at a tipping point. Our children will inherit what we leave them. As teachers and parents, it falls upon us to ensure as our kids grow into adults, they view the world with an eye missing in the past. The future depends on this.

CHAPTER FIFTY-NINE

Every Day Is Earth Day

All life is absolutely as sacred as human life.

—Thom Hartmann, *The Last Hours of Ancient Sunlight*

It's amazing what happens when you take kids to an outdoor education centre for a few days. Before the trip, they are scandalized to find out game systems, iPhones and any other form of electronic stimuli are not welcome. That's followed by great whining about having to go out in the rain, heat, cold or dark. There isn't a lot of interest in getting out into nature.

Then, over the next couple of days something very cool unfolds. Our pampered pups start to have a ball, spending their spare time playing outdoors and laying about the common room floor playing board games. The unthinkable happens, TV is forgotten.

The need to get back to nature is in all of us. It's just that it's been buried by our years in the city. Give kids a chance to muck about outdoors and before you know it, they will dig in with both hands. Without knowing it, they reconnect with the natural world.

Kudos to schools that manage to go green for a few days, once a year during Earth Week. It's important for children to be reminded about our environment and how we can fix the damage that's been done by humanity. It gives us all time to find creative ways to help revive our world. For a brief time, we touch on our connection with Mother Earth. Some schools take this a step further and make programs of conservation and awareness a part of the school lifestyle throughout of the year. Green or Eco schools are becoming the norm rather than the exception.

But touching is not enough. Our kids need to be planted into their bond with the land and with the interconnectedness of all of life. They have to be shown their rightful place in the world and the universe, and embrace a respect for our world. This is not meant to be a once a year celebration, to be later discarded, but an ongoing commitment. This mind set needn't be relegated to a few enthusiastic environmentalists joining an Eco Club. Rather, it can become so engrained into our children's make up, that caring for the Earth becomes second nature. At this point, living in harmony with the world is just the way they live.

When we're in accord with ourselves and feel at one with the Earth, we begin to act more mindfully in our everyday lives. Waste and abuse of the world become something that works outside of our way of life. When our children grasp this from their youngest days it no longer is necessary to keep trumpeting the call and sounding the alarms. They are already there. They know what they can do in their own lives, and how they can help their parents and others develop the same love and respect for nature.

Parents teach their kids by example. Many grew up in a time when there was little concern for the environment. However, once children enter school, we're able to expand their awareness and start them on a path of living in synch with their world.

For this to have true relevance we must get them out of the classroom, experiencing nature and working in the garden, feeling the soil between their fingers. By letting them interact lovingly with other living things and by telling stories from all cultures, we awaken them to their place in nature. As all of this gets woven into the daily fabric of our teaching and incorporated into the daily affairs of the school, we'll find we don't need to take out the environmental kits once a year in order to preach eco awareness.

Why are litter less lunches something reserved for Earth Week? Is a Walk to School Week necessary? In time, Earth consciousness becomes our routine. Bigger ideas flourish when we bring parents on board. When they become aware their kid's school practices conservation awareness 365 days a year, they are also likely to take a look at some of their own habits. Perhaps their younger children will arrive at their first day of school with an understanding their older siblings never had.

When it comes to implementing daily programs, such as monitoring waste, recycling and helping clean the school, from the micro world of the desk, outward to the school yard and the local neigbourhood, the older kids can take on leadership roles. Children have fertile imaginations and will be an integral part of innovative new programs and ideas.

When we are aware of our link to the Earth, we act like it. The problem is, as kids grow up in our material oriented society they forget pretty quickly. Happily, it really doesn't take a lot to remind them we are connected to each other and the planet, and our every action affects the whole. With this comes not just heightened awareness, but an awesome sense of responsibility which children will embrace. When this sense of inter-being is integrated into our lives, we begin to act more skilfully. There will never be cause to regret our actions when we act mindfully

Soon our Eco action is not separate from the main business of the school. It's a part of how the school conducts itself. From there it might spread through the community. By starting our kids green from day one, and conveying the sacred charge we have in caring for the planet, we celebrate Earth Day, every day.

CHAPTER SIXTY

The School in The Community

> We have to go back to the community and renew it.
> Then love will grow back.
>
> —Thich Naht Hahn, *Building a Community of Love*

I loved watching *Sesame Street* with my son. Of course, watching anything with your kid is amazing, but this embraced something more. First, its playful sense of humour was a refreshing change from the other kid's shows at the time. The other appeal was the sense of small town anywhere. Here was a community alive with activity, humanity and camaraderie. Everyone knew each other, and seemed genuinely glad to see them. People and Muppets worked together and helped each other through good and bad times. Pretty much everything you needed was on that street.

Contrast that to our sprawling suburbs and you see this kind of atmosphere is becoming getting harder to find each day. The sense of a living, breathing, united community has become lost as people move to the suburbs or choose to hide in fenced enclaves and high-security buildings. Local shops are being driven out of business by malls and box stores. The policeman on the beat and postal carrier are mostly strangers to the people they serve. When I see billboards trying to pass their condos and subdivisions off as communities, I cringe. In most cases they don't even come close. They're little more than clusters of houses deserted during the day, where residents hide themselves away at night. The sense of communion shows like *Sesame Street* brought to children, is little more than a fairy tale, leaving kids to feel cut off from a sense of belonging to a community.

Schools have traditionally been one of the focal points of their locale, where folks would come together to discuss local issues, meet their neighbours, or enjoy each other's company in a social setting. School was not separate from the neighbourhood, but rather an integral part of it.

Although schools do their best to maintain this position, it's largely been lost as children are dropped off and picked up at each day, as if visiting a foreign land for a few hours. School has very little involvement in local affairs and children are not always aware of what happens nearby. Parents are often afraid to let their children play outside. While it's not deliberate, kids grow up with a sense of isolation and separation from the world around them.

Schools can reconnect students with their neighbours by getting children out of the building and into the area. Residents can be invited to visit and talk with children and share their experiences. We can get involved in local matters, taking students on outings to see how businesses and other affairs are run. Volunteer programs can be implemented, in which students perform public service, where appropriate.

We may not change the neighbourhood, but we can shift our relationship with it. Our place as a focal point of the community can be re-established. By doing this, we will give children a stronger sense of involvement with the real world.

The Living School, is a community based, globally conscious school in Boulder, Colorado, which embodies these ideals. To quote their school philosophy; "A child's education is an integral part of the community, not an institution disconnected from the whole of life."

Children at the Living School not only pursue creative and academic areas to which they are naturally drawn, but learning is expanded and integrated with the whole life experience. Students become engaged in the larger population around them. The school maintains an extensive database of people and places who work with youth, teaching them skills, accepting apprentices and working with teens in the wilderness adventure program. The community and the school are considered to be one, meaning residents learn with the students. This amazing concept knocks down the walls of the school and opens them wide to everyone.

While this is a private school which is able to pursue its own mandate, it provides a living lesson about who the school should truly be trying to accommodate; its children. The Living School brings children back to that sense of belonging and being a part of a much bigger picture.

Often, this kind of school is considered experimental by mainstream education. As with other alternative schools, the public system will give a long list of objections about this kind of progressive outlook. Well perhaps it's time to stop looking down our noses and realize that it's our own system that's gone stale. By taking a deep look at how students at The Living School and other such establishments learn, we can revitalize our own teaching methods. Children can reconnect with their local area and be active participants in the world outside their schools and houses. They can become a vibrant part of their community. Like those characters on Sesame Street, they can share in a living, caring, dynamic community, and feel all the benefits.

CHAPTER SIXTY-ONE

The Value of Service

No effort in this world is lost or wasted.

—*The Bhagavad Gita: The second teaching*

Sometimes when you are struggling in your own personal issues, it's hard to imagine that others are also having problems and can use a hand. My kids often had difficulty both at school and home. This made it tough for them to see that others were suffering as well.

So during my years teaching special education I tried open up their world by finding ways we could volunteer in the community. When I discovered an organization called "Earth Rangers", a sanctuary hospital for distressed animals in the wild, I saw a goldmine of benefits for my kids. Here was a chance to offer our services and have fun at the same time. The two go together you know. Then there was the obvious advantage of getting out into the great outdoors, plus the proven therapeutic benefits of hanging out with animals.

I approached Earth Rangers and asked if they would consider waiving their age limit for volunteers, and allow us to bring our kids to their site to help out where it was needed. Being progressive thinkers, they embraced the idea and we were in.

TEACHING IN THE SPIRIT

When I told the kids we were going to help out at Earth Rangers, they were rather perplexed. They wondered aloud why we would be going out of the school to work for someone else, without getting paid. Knowing when to stop talking, I shut up and adopted a "wait and see" approach. Of course, I already knew how this would turn out.

Our first visit involved cleaning squirrel cages, and fetching branches and twigs for squirrels and raccoons to climb on during rehabilitation, before their release back into the wild. Not only did the kids have a ball with their new chores, when they returned to the main building they received a bonus. They were allowed to watch a very cool surgery being performed on a raccoon with a broken leg. Later on that year, we watched a skunk come under the knife. This produced another enthusiastic response which literally, left a lasting impression.

We spent one day each month at Earth Rangers. Every time we visited, the kids were not only learning the importance of giving back, but they were spending time surrounded by compassionate people who were dedicated to protecting and caring for those who couldn't manage. We dug gardens, fetched pine cones, washed dishes, did laundry, and performed other chores which would have appalled them had they been at home. While they were giving their time and effort, they were receiving the priceless gift of connecting with other living things, and they were shedding the weight of the city, if only briefly. I wondered if maybe later in life, one of them might want to work in nature or dedicate their time caring for animals. I never did find out. At the very least, it was a memory which would stay with them, and perhaps encourage them to pass it forward to their family, friends, and later their own children.

They looked forward to each Earth Ranger visit and as the day approached, the excitement grew. There were no academic expectations to be met here, no questions to answer, no test to be feared. This was real, living education. As it turned out, they willingly kept an Earth Rangers diary in the class.

It's part of a child's nature to want to be helpful. As a teacher you know that most kids are happy to do almost anything you ask. Unfortunately, as time goes by, attitudes begins to diminish the value of service, as people strive more and more to succeed, struggle to make ends meet, and hopefully get ahead. Service to others becomes degrading in some respects, as we teach children to be their own person, their own boss, the servant of no one.

While being independent and self-sufficient are qualities which help us survive in life, we must be sure our kids understand that a sense of responsibility to everything and everyone on this planet, gives life value and purpose. Giving to others freely and joyfully has nothing to do with submitting to "the man", living a life of resentment, or working without a sense of purpose. Meaningful service which benefits all existence and comes without strings, is one of the most liberating things we can do.

There are many organizations crying out for volunteers, and our children are a largely untapped resource. Retirement homes need children to read to seniors. Animal shelters are looking for people to come and spend time with cats or dogs waiting for adoption. Many of these organizations may be willing to have children help. Perhaps your neighbourhood has people who have simple, safe chores to be done. On a more local scale, children can help out with many of the jobs around the school which can be performed safely, with a minimum of supervision.

It requires a little imagination and flexibility on your part and the group for whom you are volunteering, but the rewards are immeasurable on both sides. The habit of giving is contagious and can carry our children into a life grounded on selflessness and compassion.

CHAPTER SIXTY-TWO

The Wisdom of The Elders

> If one has both knowledge and wisdom the lamp illuminates even the darkest night.
>
> —Chao Hsiu Chen, *The Master*

My friend's mother lived with his family until she broke her hip at the age of 95 and could no longer live safely in their two-storey home. From the time she came from Korea, she was a second mother to his children. Her simple wisdom, sense of humour and unconditional love for her grandchildren helped the family through the good and the bad times. My own grandmother lived with her daughters from the time of my granddad's premature death, until she passed away. In a simpler time with a different family dynamic, it was the norm for parents to live with their adult children and families. In many cultures it still is.

Throughout history, the elderly has held a special, often revered, place in society. They have been respected for their life experience and the wisdom which often comes with age. Senior members of the family have played a huge role in the education and rearing of children. Younger inexperienced parents were grateful for the insight and care offered by those who had travelled further along the path. Cultural rituals and time-honoured stories were passed down through the generations by those who valued their traditions. It was to the most experienced members of the tribe that members would come in times of uncertainty. Elders would frequently be the decision makers in the community and their ideas were respected and valued. Children benefited from the wisdom, love, and experience these cherished relatives provided.

In more recent times, as the pace of life has quickened, there's been a gradual makeover of attitudes. As technology and acquired knowledge become more important, the opinions and contributions of the elderly have been devalued. Seniors are not always esteemed by society. They are often deemed too slow, too feeble, and usually too set in their ways to keep pace with the demands of our material oriented world. As adults, we're too busy trying to get ahead and keep up with the pace to pander to them. We don't have the time or the resources to have them living in our homes. So the elderly are increasing left to fend for themselves or to be cared for by others.

It's here where our kids also lose out. They don't always have the same access to the prudence of the experienced members of our society. This can cut them off from many of the traditions of their cultures. They miss the stories, the perspective and the love the children of earlier generations took for granted. In a society where youth is valued and age is feared, our children miss the tempering aspect the truly mature are able to provide. Without this knowledge and softening effect of experience, there is little to help balance the hard edge today's life imposes.

Many parents find it increasingly difficult to raise their children in an effective and positive way, simply because they themselves don't have the skill and firsthand familiarity with life our elders may have. Emotionally, some mothers and fathers are little more than children themselves, barely able to manage their own lives, never mind raising the young.

Having a large number of years under your belt is no guarantee that you have earned your badge of wisdom, but it's a given the young can learn much from the more seasoned. Values such as humility, selflessness and humour are generally those qualities which are acquired over time, alongside the many battle scars.

This is why it makes so much sense to start welcoming seniors into our schools. Although some schools do have a senior volunteer program, there are many children who are moving on in their lives without the benefit of guidance from those with more life experience. Having our own elders come into our schools to provide nurturing to the younger children, and insight to older students who are developing their own views of the world, is a gift we owe to our youth. Seniors with unique histories can be invited to share them on special occasions such as Remembrance Day. Others, who are able, might come into the school to volunteer on a regular basis.

Teachers and support workers are harassed with curriculum expectations and the demands of large class sizes. This means the nurturing care which kids need so badly may be falling by the wayside. Having older adults in our schools could help provide them with much of what is currently lacking in their lives. It also would give children a new perspective on not only the elderly, but on the entire process of aging and life. Children can learn that old age is just another phase of life, a stage which can be just as rewarding as youth, adolescence or adulthood. It can become one more way of helping them embrace the entire spectrum of life.

This also has the benefit of giving the seniors who come into the lives of our children a new lease on life, a sense of purpose.

As educators and caregivers, we cannot help but improve the quality of our children's lives when we invite our seniors into our schools to share their gifts.

CHAPTER SIXTY-THREE

The Mind and The Media

It is a miracle that curiosity survives formal education.

—Albert Einstein

Guess which place is guaranteed to have the longest line at any food court? No, it's not the salad place, the Italian or the Asian. Sorry, you've had your chances. The correct answer is, McDonalds. Take your kids to any mall and that's where most of them will want to eat. Why? Is it the quality of the food? For us, that's likely the first consideration. Maybe it's the cheapest? Another thought, but you're stilling missing the mark. The answer is none of the above. The truth is, people eat at McDonalds because McDonalds tells them to. Commercials hammer the message home from the time kids start watching, and their media gurus are good at their job. By the time they can make an informed and independent choice, their brains have already stepped into autopilot and sent them off to the arches.

Media has this profound effect on everyone. Although they would be loath to admit it, people run much of their lives in accordance to what they take in through advertising. Witness the number of people driving in cars too big for them to handle, or the individuals who walk around like zombies punching out text messages on their phones. People line up at fast food places to consume food they know does them no good. They've become so brainwashed they do these things without even thinking. It's just natural to have an SUV, the latest high-tech phone, the best home theatre and to eat KFC. The media dishes it out and everyone laps it up.

Children are the most susceptible to media bombardment. As they watch their three to five hours of television a day, they are assaulted with hundreds of messages, all telling them what they should want and how they should live. They are constantly seeing lifestyle shows and videos which portray false images about life. Style is important. Money is what we strive for. Convenience is paramount.

Just take a look at many of the music videos and commercials. Everything is about lifestyle; having the coolest car, looking buff and being surrounded by all the material world has to offer. Have all this and you have success. This is our mission in life. We realize early that happiness is sold out there, and later on we learn what we need to do to get it.

So is it our job to handle this? We could turn the other way and hope someone else will deal with it. We might just try to brush off the messages and outlaw violence and sexual content from our schools. But this solves nothing. What we need to do is take the time to look at messages and dialogue with young people about them. If kids are going to understand the ideas they're being sold are just a mirage, they have to be able to step back and examine what's being pitched. To do this, they need someone to help them look objectively at what's being preached and the motivation behind it.

The illusions which are being portrayed need to come under the microscope so kids can make an informed examination of their validity. There's a caution here. When you step into this it's important not get onto your soap box. Kids don't need any missionaries. We aren't here to judge. Instead, together we're considering what we're seeing and hearing, and then discussing their validity. Chances are, when kids look carefully, they will start to see the holes in these messages, on their own.

By doing this, young people can see beyond the simple picture being shown on the screen, or the lyrics they are hearing, and truly get to the core of those offerings. Is there anything wrong with partying and hanging out with girls in cars? Not really, despite what your mother told you. Is there a problem with being rich? Not necessarily. Is it a driving force in your life? Does it guarantee success and lasting happiness? These questions might need a little more reflection.

Kids will continue to view films and play games which offer increasing amounts of carnage. We don't need to rehash the endless studies involving the relationship between violent games and shows, and life attitudes here. As teachers, we know and see all too well the affect they have on our kids, and when we're concerned about a student we have an obligation to make the parents aware. We may need to coach them on making some firm decisions at home. However, the fact is, kids will continue to be exposed to this skewed view of life. As instructors and mentors, we are totally remiss if we simply bemoan the fact that our kids are being damaged by it all. This doesn't help anyone, nor does trashing it in front of them.

What we can do to make a difference, is welcome these themes into the classroom and take a long, hard look at what we're all being exposed to. Record some particularly persuasive commercials and bring them for the class to view. Open up discussion. Engage in an exchange with the kids. Ask them to look impartially at the product. Can they discern need from luxury? Can they pinpoint who is profiting from this advertising? How does this affect the average person who's coerced into buying stuff that is either too expensive or dangerous? Take a deep look at the history of the cigarette industry. Here is the classic example of media brainwashing which has led to the death of millions. There's an endless list of similar examples.

Another activity which kids will find challenging and fun at the same time, is stripping down commercials. You can show your students several television ads and then ask them to take away all the drama, glitz and suggestions and determine what the actual message is. For example, a deodorant commercial may show a smartly dressed, successful woman going to meetings all day, and then dancing at a party in the evening surrounded by good looking men. What is the real message? Our deodorant will keep you dry. Now have the kids talk about all the other stories which surround the ad. It's amazing how they'll see through all the hype being pushed at the public in an effort to sell a product. This is a good way for them to see how companies are mostly selling an image to get people to buy what they are selling.

Remember that awareness is the key. Most consumers are not wholly conscious of what they're taking in. It's exciting and visually stimulating, so they watch. Meanwhile, the messages they are receiving are shaping their view of the world in a much deeper place.

What you may have thought to be inappropriate for the classroom can provide amazing opportunities to explore outlooks together, and start kids looking at what they see and hear in a new and critical way. As professionals you know where to draw the line. At the very least, students will be more aware of the messages they are receiving, and maybe somewhere along the way, they will start to take a second look with a clear eye.

Older kids in particular, will relish the chance to share their entertainment choices; and once they start critically examining these choices, they will show an insight that many adults might not expect. It's a matter of bringing awareness to young people rather than condemning or prohibiting. This isn't a matter of right or wrong, bad or good. Our students cannot or will not avoid the media blitz, but if they are able to look carefully and objectively, they are much less likely to be conned into and controlled by it.

CHAPTER SIXTY-FOUR

Rewiring the Brain

> New habits arise because old habits are blocked.
>
> —Rupert Sheldrake, *The Presence of The Past: Morphic Resonance and The Habits Of Nature*

In the thought provoking movie *What the Bleep Do We Know?* there's a brilliant scene at a wedding, where a woman is moaning about how she always spills drinks on her dress and is forever having accidents. During the next few scenes these things soon become self-fulfilling prophecies, as she stumbles from one disaster to another. More than a few people I know said they could see a part of themselves in this scene.

"I always do that." "I'm so clumsy." "Stupid me." "I'm always late." "It won't work for me, it never does." Do these assertions sound familiar? If you take notice, I think you'll find people spend a lot of time in such self-deprecating talk. There are reasons we act like this. First, it gets us a lot of attention. Secondly, it's very likely this is the way we've thought all our lives, and it hasn't helped being around like-minded people. Our brain and our body are obedient servants and you can be sure they will do their best to turn these statements into reality.

TEACHING IN THE SPIRIT

"As a man thinketh, so is he." Jesus understood Quantum Physics, long before Schroedinger thought about gassing his cat. We continually create our reality. Every day and every moment we reinforce beliefs, and the sorry part is it doesn't do us one bit of good. Every time we feed our brains lies about who we are, all the electrical impulses leap to attention and loop back to solidify those ideas. Seeds are then planted which can ripen into that particular reality. We keep telling ourselves we are clumsy and sure enough we find ourselves tripping over things and dropping expensive glassware.

Convince yourself you're always late, and it doesn't matter how much extra time you allow for an appointment, something will come along to delay you. You've written your own script. Believe me, it's a habit I still slip into far too often.

While some people are lucky enough to discover these patterns in their adult years, many will never have this secret revealed. Still others will refuse to believe it is true, no matter what the evidence. It flies in the face of everything we've heard our entire lives. Accidents happen, right? It's just coincidence. I would never sabotage myself.

We've heard people cry that life is tough, and some folks get the good cards and others go bust. Religions try to convince us that we're mere pawns in some cosmic game of chess and the best we can do is play the cards we're dealt. When things go wrong we're victims, and there isn't a whole lot to do about it. If we work at it hard enough, this becomes our belief system and that's when the trouble starts.

Now, imagine what would happen if we were to learn early in life that we needn't be playing this game. Suppose we realized in our childhood we really did have a choice about how our lives were going to turn out.

The next obstacle we would probably have to overcome is the adults who constantly pepper us with their negativity.

"You're always doing that."

"She is so...."

"It doesn't surprise me one bit."

"I told you that would happen."

This list is endless and the more we hear it, the more we believe. As I walk through schools and visit classrooms, I frequently hear damaging phrases like these being tossed out by unthinking adults. And the kids lap it up. In fact, they're likely to oblige their teacher by proving them right in short order.

Then we have the nerve to tell kids to make better choices. I don't mean the kind of choice such as not putting gum in Suzie's hair or eating play dough. How about the option not to be the playground punching bag or the choice not to be the kid who is so clumsy no one wants her to be on their team?

By the time he reaches school, your child may already have these habits set. But don't despair. The situation is completely reversible. We can start to break the belief cycle and give him some real choices about who he is. It starts with being very mindful and awake; listening and watching for the signs that he's sending himself false signals. If you're alert, you'll see the clues that someone is in a dangerous loop, one that could last a lifetime. At this point, you have the chance to help break the cycle.

We too are not so old we can't break free from the blueprint. Our most powerful ally is mindfulness. When we find ourselves falling into an old mould which drags us down, we need to stop, take a break, and observe what we're doing and how we're acting. That awareness immediately puts the brakes on old thinking. Then we can re-direct our thoughts into something which fits more into our own design for life. This isn't an overnight affair, but by being constantly wakeful and on our guard, we can start changing what our brain expects, and start taking control of our lives. We are then no longer the victim of a cold, impersonal world, or even worse, a spiteful angry God.

Now we have that all sorted, we're equipped to start helping our kids come to the same realization. After that, they can apply this in their own lives.

When you catch children in this sort of self-deprecating cycle, please gently redirect them. Help them realize a mistake does not equal stupidity; a missed ball isn't the same as clumsy and a bad decision does not equal a bad kid. I've often given kids a sort of confidence building mantra such as "I'm a good kid," simply to put the brakes to the thought train and allow them to come back to who they are. It isn't the actual words which are so important; rather it's the act of short circuiting the old patterns. When you see a situation which concerns you, make the other staff conscious of what you've noticed and get them on board to support the child. Keep an eye out to make sure other children are not reinforcing the old loop. Perhaps their friends can add their support. Kids will step up when you remind them they are all in this together. Please don't be afraid to approach a colleague if you notice he is constantly putting kids down. He may not like it, but you might get him thinking.

Every day, have your kids reflect on their higher qualities. Constantly remind them that what they think or say is stored in their minds, like a computer, and as the old saying goes, "Garbage in, garbage out." Help parents realize how important it is to reinforce this at home. It's vital to their child's future.

Children can understand they do have control over the way they act or are perceived by others. By reprogramming those self-destructive words and thoughts the brain in essence, is being re-wired. When this happens, real lifestyle choices can be made. When the mind is no longer mired in the old damaging thought circuit, it has the ability to choose what works best. If children discover this wonderful, liberating truth early in their lives, they will have the chance to truly be the captain of their own ship.

Now this, not having the best test results or the straightest line, is something to celebrate.

For centuries we've stumbled along in the outdated belief we basically are who we are or that we have to fight to make a change. However, this isn't the case. Most of who we think we are is a construct we've been building throughout our entire lives. We re-create ourselves in every moment, and since this is a fact, we would do well to listen to what avatars and masters have told us throughout history. "As a man thinketh, so is he."

CHAPTER SIXTY-FIVE

The Power of Touch

> Touch is the most intimate of our senses, and in reaching out to others, the message is clear; I'm here, I'm close and I care.
>
> —Leo Buscaglia, *Bus Nine to Paradise*

Your child falls down and runs into the house in tears. You ask what's wrong and she points to a slightly skinned knee. While at first, she is inconsolable, wise doctor that you are, you clean the wound with a wet cloth, add a colourful bandage, kiss her on the cheek and tell her you love her. Miracle cure!

A simple touch can stop a baby's tears. A hand on the shoulder can make a heart-breaking sports defeat easier to take. It can let an elderly relative know that they are still cared for and valued. Healing touch or Reiki can alleviate chronic pain and distress. We all need human contact and without it, something magic is missing from our lives.

Unfortunately, touch has become completely taboo in our schools. Teachers should not touch students and of course children must never touch each other. The reason for this is simple. Touch has been used so improperly over the years that now it has a bad rap. In our society, many troubled adults have abused children in their search for some kind of distorted gratification. Out of their own needs for attention or revenge, many children have wrongfully accused their educators of sexual harassment. Add into that mix a few dozen lawyers with dollar signs in their eyes and the climate of fear is cultivated.

Adults have taken advantage of their superior strength and position of authority to cruelly punish young people. Angered youths have attacked their instructors, and the incidence of youths committing violent acts against their peers is spiraling of control. Small wonder touching is equated with trouble.

Law books are full of cases about teachers who have been witch-hunted for innocent and well-intentioned contact. The solution to all of this as usual, is to take the easy way out and impose a total prohibition against all human contact, at school or in the workplace.

The problem with all of this is that by eliminating touch, and creating a climate of fear and negativity around it, we are denying one of the most basic of human needs. In fact, we're making our children afraid of physical contact. Yet countless studies have proved infants who are given the warmth of loving human contact, thrive over those denied this gift.

Now, it goes without saying our kids need to be wary of inappropriate or unwanted touching, and they need to learn how to handle unacceptable conduct. However, driven by the media and our litigious society, we have created an exaggerated sense of paranoia among adults, and as is inevitable, passed it on to our kids. As it so often happens in this world, hysteria trumps balance.

I'm a *huggy* person. I'm never been afraid to embrace a child who I knew was hurting. Why? Because it's the most naturally healing thing you can do. A gentle touch on the shoulder or pat on the back, when it comes from caring and compassion, can do wonders for a child, especially if they come from a non-demonstrative household. When it comes from the heart, touch is a wonderful, comforting tool. When colleagues have told me of their personal veto on touching, I've made it clear that if I was ever given a prohibition from this integral part of interaction with kids, I would rather leave the profession.

However, there are other caveats. We need to remember we are made of energy, which we constantly release. When we touch out of anger or lust, that energy is passed on to the receiver. That is the reason we recoil at the touch of certain individuals. We feel that energy in our field even before the physical contact is made. Always keep this in mind when working closely with others. Go back to being the observer and get a handle on how you're feeling, because we have no right to pass on negativity to others, even unwittingly. Learning more about therapeutic touch, such as Reiki, can help us to use touch as an instrument of healing.

So how do we handle this issue? First, it's not with a carte blanche to start hugging and holding everyone with whom we make contact. Many people, for whatever reason, have an aversion to touch. Their reasons are all legitimate, no matter what we may think, and we have to respect them. Many parents have also been scared into censuring all forms of touch between adult and child. Administrators also frown upon physical contact because of the potential repercussions. and after all you have to work within the parameters of the workplace.

In the end, if you appreciate your own comfort zone and that of each child, you will be able to instinctively know when a pat on the shoulder, a rub on the head, or even a hug is warranted. We all have enough sense to keep ourselves out of situations where we can be compromised and must always be vigilant. But we should never shy away from human contact out of fear. Tread lightly, and remember that a rather sordid history of wrongful touching has left a bad taste. So you have to always be conscious of your personal intentions, and at the same time remember the value of human contact, when it comes straight from the heart.

CHAPTER SIXTY-SIX

When School Becomes Home

Home is Where the Heart Is.

—Pliny the Elder

Although the basic school set up hasn't changed that much since I was a kid, the dynamics surrounding the school day have. For starters, I went home for lunch. As I came through the door, mum asked me what I wanted to eat, if it wasn't already on the table. She would grab herself something and join me at the table or in front of the Flintstones. After a nice hour together, I would reluctantly head back to class. This isn't a Disney family fantasy. It was the norm. Nearly all of my friends had the same kind of experience. Few kids didn't have someone to greet them home at noon. At five or six o'clock, most of us could set their clock by the time dad would walk through the door.

Evenings were often spent playing games, watching TV as a family or just talking. Mum would usually send me off to school in the morning with a good breakfast in my belly, generally feeling all was right with the world. It's not surprising I didn't particularly want to go to school. I certainly didn't understand why I had to. School was okay I suppose, but home was much better.

When School Becomes Home

Flash forward into the 21st century and you'll find a major shift in life styles. There may be no one to see you off in the morning, or greet you when you get home. Lunch is likely out of a container or bag and eaten in the school lunch room. Usually both parents are working, and keeping long and odd hours at that, so that kids are often home alone. Many children get themselves up, splash down something they call breakfast and head out on their own, often returning to an empty house, along with strict instructions not to go out, answer the door, or even pick up the telephone. Increasing numbers of homes are run by a single parent who is trying to keep a job, manage the house and take care of the kids.

Evenings may consist of little more than a repeated diet of fast food, TV, video games and computers. If mum and dad are around, there's a good chance they're busy with their own homework or chores which keep them at a distance.

This scenario may seem very grim, and although it may not be universal, it's a reality in a lot of households today. For many children, home is not always the nurturing, loving or even stimulating place is once was. Ask a room full of kids what they did over the holidays and a startling number will say "nothing." To elaborate, nothing means they played video games, went online and generally just hung out around the house. There are neighbourhoods where kids don't even get outside to play with their friends, because their parents don't feel it safe for them do so.

While there are still many children fortunate enough to

have a supportive and inspiring home life, sadly it isn't always the case. The fallout from this is predictable. When the home situation is not up to par, then school becomes the surrogate. If that environment is unstable, uninspired or unpredictable, school offers everything that is the opposite. There are friends to play with, things to do, and adults who on the whole, are caring and interested in what they are doing. In essence, school has become a substitute home for many kids. It fills a gap which is missing in their lives and they're eager to be there.

This means we need to adjust our way of thinking. We must be alert to the fact that our old ideas about the value of school, and our old notions about kid's attitudes towards school may no longer hold true. Whereas school used to be a place we went to learn, whether we liked it or not, it has now become much more than that. It fills needs that are not always being met outside. There is stability, reliability and camaraderie. There is physical and mental stimulation, plus challenge. For some children it may be the only time during the day when they feel safe, secure and wanted.

When we see things from this point of view, we're a bit more careful how we deal with kids. Remembering that for some, school may be the one bright light in a rather grim existence, we are ever mindful of our words and attitudes. Since the school family may be substituting for a stable home life, it's crucial to keep that life interesting and motivating. Where there is a void, we need to do our best to fill it.

Some educators will still insist that a school's sole mandate is to give kids the education they need for their future, full stop. They'll argue that the balance of a child's upbringing rests in the hands of the parents. If there was ever a basis for this belief, it doesn't hold much truth today. We can't hide from this huge responsibility. Values we previously assumed were being acquired at home need to be taught and modelled at school, because in many cases when kids come to us, they are truly coming home.

CHAPTER SIXTY-SEVEN

Who Do We Think They Are?

> Everyone is born with different gifts, for which their parents are not responsible.
>
> —Chao-Hsim Chen, *The Master*

Certain words are taboo, especially in school; mostly ones you wouldn't say around your maiden aunts. Yet there is very benign sounding word constantly used in school which can do a lot more damage. The word is "should". Bet you didn't see that coming. Just see how we use it to degrade children. "Well, Johnny *should* know better than to do that." "You *should* know your French verbs." "I *should* be able to leave you for a moment without you doing this." "They *should* be able to handle these expectations by now." The list of "shoulds" is endless. Walk into any discussion about children and you will hear the word used as if kids were some kind of device which wasn't working properly.

Should is one of the most overused words in the English language, along with its flip side shouldn't. People should and shouldn't their way through life, as if there was someone keeping score. Teachers have a two-fold use for the word "should." They use the word to catalogue the behaviours that make them happy. In addition, should is the term used when a child doesn't meet their own personal standards. Should for the most part is partnered with disappointment, as in "You should know better. You should be finished by now."

Should often suggests there is an ideal child who reaches each stage of development on the date experts have decided is the norm. Anyone who doesn't measure up obviously has something wrong with them. Now, while there are certain gauges for a child's growth and times to be concerned that perhaps all is not well, this quest for so called normalcy often blinds us to the fact that each kid is unique. Everyone isn't heading in the same direction, nor have they travelled a similar route to where they are now. Yes, we need to be aware when a child is in jeopardy, but we mustn't be preoccupied with statistics, research, judgments and expectations.

As adult and especially as educators, we are pleased to see our kids acquire qualities like intelligence, honesty, imagination, humour, compassion and fairness. Remember, these are just pieces of the whole. There is no model child. There will always be something we feel the need to moan about. However, we have to remember, all of us contain the seeds of all facets of humanness. Our task is not to build the perfect child. That's already been done. What we are striving for is to bring children to a sense of knowing who they are, so they are able to naturally find the best path for themselves and others.

By trying to hold them up to some sort of ideal, we're missing the child for who he is. Many of the oddities which annoy teachers may be the very signs of someone destined to become a vibrant, creative person, unbound by the standards we may have set for her. The artist, the career sports person, the foreign correspondent, all have different qualities which will be a part of their future. Maybe none of them will reach the bar we set for them. There is no mould, so we have to stop looking for one.

By all means aspire to see the best emerge from each child you deal with, but please don't try to make them conform to your image of the ideal student. When you start comparing, you are in for a personal disappointment. More damaging is the harm you do to the child who is starting to find himself. Try to avoid using the word "should" when you evaluate. It really is quite irrelevant in most cases. You might as well say, "It's April and it shouldn't be snowing." Guess what? It is and we have to deal with it.

There's no point in lamenting what should or shouldn't be. Instead, move ahead and take the kids where you can. Instead of telling a child what he should be doing, you can say, "I know maybe some of the other kids may be able to do that. But you know what? You haven't got there yet. Maybe we just need some more time." You get the idea.

Yes, we want our kids to be the best version of themselves they can be, but please don't try to make them into someone else. Be mindful that your vision of what a child should or shouldn't be may be your own invention. In reality that person does not exist.

CHAPTER SIXTY-EIGHT

The Word Is Not Reality

> For thought is a bird of space, that in a cage of words may indeed unfold its wings but cannot fly.
>
> —Kahlil Gibran, *The Prophet*

Words can be beautiful. A play on the English language, a cleverly contrived phrase, a descriptive passage which has the capacity to pull the reader into the author's world of feeling and sense; all are a form of art. There are masters of prose and poetry who write as if their words flowed directly from the universe. Some writers can change our mood and feelings with a simple expression penned from the heart. Others make us laugh out loud.

Certain words are used to convey a message. In the case of this book, they were chosen to help you the reader, consider there is an alternative, better way to serve youth.

It goes without saying teaching requires using our words. We speak to our kids, they in turn to us and their peers; and we prod and push them to put words to paper. We are constantly referring to written texts. Words are an integral part of each day.

However, there is a caution here. We need to reflect for a moment about why we use our words. Are we using them to communicate or fill awkward silences? Do they impart knowledge? Are we attempting to decode reality? Is manipulation our goal? Do we just love to hear ourselves speak? Whatever our reasons, we have to ask ourselves whether we are overloading our kids with talk. Does all this chatter help them experience reality? Are words a substitute for true life experience?

Words are not reality. They are merely tools used to convey meaning to our world. Often, they fall far short of the mark. We're so frequently lost in our words and conversations we often completely miss what is happening right in front of us.

As teachers, we need to be constantly aware of this and strive to make our children's experiences as genuine and vital as they can be. A lesson about plants is not the same as feeling the soil and smelling the flowers. A poem about a child walking through the forest cannot compare to actually passing through the trees, seeing, hearing and smelling the sensations.

As you move through the day, ask yourself if there is a way you can help children experience the world directly, rather than just handing them jargon from a page, or showing a video on the Smartboard. Words have their beauty and are a bridge to the fantastic. However, they are not reality and can never be a substitute for what is real.

JUST ONE MORE THING

The End Is the Beginning

> Every sincere effort is recognized in the divine consciousness.
>
> —Paramhansa Yogananda, *Writings on Effort*

History is filled with the stories of sages who have told us there's a better way to live. Out there beyond the material greed, the grasping, the personal dramas and manufactured stories, is something we all know the truth of, but mostly ignore. What we do know, is that we are much more than our simple selves can conceive. What we think we are, is largely a construct, a personal self we've spent our entire lives creating, until we believe that's all there is to ourselves. If we can lift the veil and open to this knowing, then we can shake ourselves out of our small ego centered existence, into the richness of being. It's never too late to begin, but it cannot happen until we are so honest with ourselves that we start to burn for something more.

Children have an advantage. They haven't had as many years to become mired in self-importance and indulgence as we older folk have. So logically, it would seem that if we, as supposedly wiser adults, help them find that better way of life when they are young, they have a chance of rediscovering it. The problem is, we're either stuck in our insistence that we are stellar examples of lives well lived, or we don't know how to begin. So for the most part, we wash our hands and leave it to others, fate or time to do the job; and we just blunder through, missing the most wonderful opportunities to explore life together.

And so, education continues to be little more than an information factory, a training ground for the workforce. Byzantine curriculum and report cards, which a linguist would have trouble deciphering, are celebrated as being progressive. Rubrics are needed to have the kids write their names and the most ludicrous part is, it's done under the guise of creating a better quality of education, smarter kids and a brighter future. The sad truth is, while the authors of our education system keep changing the way we deliver curriculum to kids, they miss the greatest gift education has to offer; self-discovery.

Nothing we teach our kids is worth a toss, as long as they have no conception of who and what they are; and what life has to offer. We continually deceive our kids into believing we are leading them along the path to success and happiness. In this, we do them the greatest disservice.

I have known some wonderful, compassionate and caring teachers whose hands were constantly shackled by the system in which they worked. Having to stand by and watch this charade masked as learning, led to a few sleepless nights and many moments of frustration during my career. Writing down my observations and feelings became very cathartic, but it changed nothing. Then the notion came that perhaps there were a lot of others who felt the same way, and were looking for a new way to do what they love, but in a way, they know is honest. Given this direction, aggravation and irritation turned into inspiration.

Of course, I then needed to rid myself of the self-doubt, the impudence it takes for a mere teacher to question generations of tradition. By what authority do I have the right to say we're doing it wrong and need to start changing the way we look at education? After all, look at all those successful graduates we produce every year. Surely that's proof that we are running an accomplished educational program? What about all the research and papers by experts? Nevertheless, when you open your eyes wide and expand your mind, you see things very differently.

TEACHING IN THE SPIRIT

The evidence that all is not well is all around us. Maybe we're oblivious to it all because we're wrapped up in trying to get through our days, rather than celebrate them. Perhaps we have so many toys that we're sedated, fooled into believing this is the good life, one our children should be inheriting.

It would have been easy to turn this into condemnation of everything we are doing in education, one tirade after another, passing judgment on everyone and everything in the system. Trust me, it's been done before and it serves no one.

Through all that is lacking and misdirected in our education system, honour, compassion and dedication are still all around us. Even the smallest flame can't be quenched by the flood of bureaucracy and arrogance which now poisons the system.

My motivation still rests in the knowledge that if we untie all the knots, and the tangles of deception, we can help kids see how amazing life can be.

True and meaningful and lasting change does not happen through anger and bitterness. It comes from openness, compassion, and allowing life to unfold naturally. Violent revolution and war are based on outrage, and while the changes they bring about can be sudden and earth shattering, they don't endure because they have no foundation. The changes which come from true insight are subtler. They don't necessarily start with a big bang, but once they begin, they ripple to the horizon. They abide because their base is rooted in honesty and truth.

As we move towards a new paradigm in our teaching, we would do well to be mindful of these things. Remember, every step, no matter how small, when it comes from a place of compassion and awareness, is one that will take our world in the right direction. This takes a lot of patience, because our instinct is to the leap into the fray with both guns blazing, armed with a righteousness belief we can single headedly save humanity. We are not evangelists. The world does not need to be saved. It does however, need to leave its collective dream and wake up.

This is not so much a change as a metamorphosis. Like the caterpillar, everything that is needed for transformation is already here. Our role as teachers is to act on the spiritual DNA, taking what is already known, and helping with the makeover.

The End Is the Beginning

There is no timeline, which is good, because you will drive yourself crazy waiting for it to happen. Rather, it's a process, which once started, is irreversible because it is based on truth. The caterpillar is comfortable being a caterpillar, but one day it must become a butterfly. So the best thing to do is to give nature a good nudge, then let it take its course, and sit back and enjoy the ride.

About the Author

Stephen F.C. Porter spent twenty years working with special students in the public education system. Prior to that he was a producer on talk radio during which time he wrote, directed and produced a documentary examining what motivates children to leave their homes and live on the street. Stephen stresses the need to teach the "whole child" and believes our approach to education needs to shift its focus to one which fosters free thinking and self-awareness.

www.ingramcontent.com/pod-product-compliance
Lightning Source LLC
Chambersburg PA
CBHW070422010526
44118CB00014B/1863